Mrs. Johnson

Differentiating Instruction With Menus

Science

MIDDLE SCHOOL EDITION

Differentiating Instruction With Menus

Science

Laurie E. Westphal

PRUFROCK PRESS INC.
WACO, TEXAS

ISBN-13: 978-1-59363-368-4
ISBN-10: 1-59363-368-8

Prufrock Press Inc.
P.O. Box 8813
Waco, TX 76714-8813
Phone: (800) 998-2208
Fax: (800) 240-0333
http://www.prufrock.com

Many thanks to Diane McVeigh,
the "unofficial" mentor who adopted me
during my first year teaching and talked me down
many times during those fifth and sixth science years!

CONTENTS

Part 1
All About Choice and Menus

CHAPTER 1

Choice

"Oh my gosh! THAAAAANK YOU!" exclaimed one of my students as he fell to his knees dramatically in the middle of my classroom. I had just handed out a list menu on the periodic table and told my class they would be able to choose how they wanted to learn the material.

Why Is Choice Important to Middle School Students?

> " . . . Almost every kid in middle school wants freedom of his or her choice of what they want to work on. They just do."
>
> —Eighth-grade math student

First, we have to consider who (or what) our middle school students personify. During these years, adolescents struggle to determine who they are and how they fit into the world around them. They constantly try new ideas (the hydrogen peroxide in the hair sounded like a good idea at the time), new experiences (if you sit on the second-floor roof of your home one more time, I will tell your parents!), and constant flux of personalities (preppy one day, dark nails and lipstick the next) in order to obtain "zen" and find themselves. During this process, which can take from a few months to a few years depending on the child, academics are not always at the forefront of his mind unless the student has chosen that as part of his identity. Knowing this, instruction and higher level products have to engage the individuals these students are trying to become.

"I like choice because I get to make decisions on my own. For myself!"

—Seventh-grade science student

Ask adults whether they would prefer to choose what to do or be told what to do, and of course, they are going to say they would prefer to have a choice. Students have the same feelings, especially middle school students. Academics usually have been pushed back in priority as they seek to find themselves, so implementing choice as a way to engage these students has many explicit benefits once it has been developed as the center of high-level thinking.

"I like being able to choose, because I can pick what I am good at and avoid my weaknesses."

—Eighth-grade language arts student

One benefit of choice is its ability to meet the needs of so many different students and their learning styles. The Dunedin College of Education (Keen, 2001) conducted a research study on the preferred learning styles of 250 gifted students. Students were asked to rank different learning options. Of the 13 different options described to the students, only one option did not receive at least one negative response, and that was the option of having a choice. Although all students have different learning styles and preferences, choice is the one option that can meet everyone's needs. Unlike elementary students, middle school students have been engaged in the learning process long enough that they usually can recognize their own strengths and weaknesses, as well their learning styles. By allowing choice, students are able to choose what best fits their learning styles and educational needs.

> "... I am different in the way I do stuff. I like to build stuff with my hands more than other things."
>
> *—Sixth-grade student*

Another benefit of choice is a greater sense of independence for the students. What a powerful feeling! Students will be designing and creating a product based on what they envision, rather than what their teacher envisions. When students would enter my middle school classroom, they often had been trained by previous teachers to produce exactly what the teacher wanted, not what the students thought would be best. Teaching my students that what they envision could be correct (and wonderful) was a struggle. "Is this what you want? or "Is this right?" were popular questions as we started the school year. Allowing students to have choices in the products they create to show their learning helps create independence at an early age.

> "It [choice] puts me in a good mood to participate!"
>
> *—Seventh-grade student*

Strengthened student focus on the required content is a third benefit. Middle school students already have begun to transition from an academic focus to more of a social one. Choice is a way to help bring their focus back to the academic aspect of school. When students have choices in the activities they wish to complete, they are more focused on the learning that leads to their choice product. Students become excited when they learn information that can help them develop a product they would like to create. Students will pay close attention to instruction and have an immediate application for the knowledge being presented in class. Also, if students are focused, they are less likely to be off task during instruction.

Many a great educator has referred to the idea that the best learning takes place when the students have a desire to learn. Some middle school students still have a desire to learn anything that is new to them, but many others do not want to learn anything unless it is of interest to them. By incorporating different activities from which to choose, students stretch beyond what they already know, and teachers create a void that needs to be filled. This void leads to a desire to learn.

How Can Teachers Provide Choices?

> "The GT students seem to get more involved in assignments when they have choice. They have so many creative ideas and the menus give them the opportunity to use them."
>
> *—Social studies teacher*

When people go to a restaurant, the common goal is to find something on the menu to satisfy their hunger. Students come into our classrooms having a hunger as well—a hunger for learning. Choice menus are a way of allowing our students to choose how they would like to satisfy that hunger. At the very least, a menu is a list of choices that students use to choose an activity (or activities) they would like to complete to show what they have learned. At best, it is a complex system in which students earn points by making choices from different areas of study. All menus also should incorporate a free-choice option for those "picky eaters" who would like to place a special order to satisfy their learning hunger.

Tic-Tac-Toe Menu

> "They [Tic-Tac-Toe Menus] can be a real pain. A lot of times I only liked two of the choices and had to do the last one. Usually I got stuck with a play or presentation."
>
> *—Sixth-grade math student (asked to step out of her comfort zone based on the tic-tac-toe design)*

Description

The Tic-Tac-Toe menu (see Figure 1.1) is a basic menu with a total of eight predetermined choices and one free choice for students. All choices are created at the same level of Bloom's Revised taxonomy (Anderson et al., 2001). All carry the same weight for grading and have similar expectations for completion time and effort.

Benefits

Flexibility. This menu can cover one topic in depth, or three different objectives. When this menu covers just one objective, students have the option of completing three products in a tic-tac-toe pattern, or simply picking three from the menu. When it covers three objectives, students will need to complete a tic-tac-toe pattern (one in each column or row) to be sure they have completed one activity from each objective.

Friendly Design. Students quickly understand how to use this menu.

Weighting. All products are equally weighted, so recording grades and maintaining paperwork is easily accomplished with this menu.

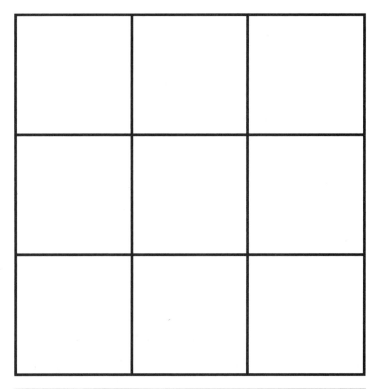

Figure 1.1. Tic-tac-toe menu.

Limitations

Few Topics. These menus only cover one or three topics.

Short Time Period. They are intended for shorter periods of time, between 1–3 weeks.

Student Compromise. Although this menu does allow choice, a student will sometimes have to compromise and complete an activity he or she would not have chosen because it completes his or her tic-tac-toe. (This is not always bad, though!)

Time Considerations

These menus usually are intended for shorter amounts of completion time—at the most, they should take 3 weeks. If it focuses on one topic in-depth, the menu could be completed in one week.

List Menu

"I like that you can add up the points to be over 100, so even if you make some small mistakes, your grade could still be a 100."

—Seventh-grade student

Description

The List Menu (see Figure 1.2), or Challenge List, is a more complex menu than the Tic-Tac-Toe Menu, with a total of at least 10 predetermined choices, each with its own point value, and at least one free choice for students. Choices are simply listed with assigned points based on the levels of Bloom's Revised taxonomy. The choices carry different weights and have different expectations for completion time and effort. A point criterion is set forth that equals 100%, and students choose how they wish to attain that point goal.

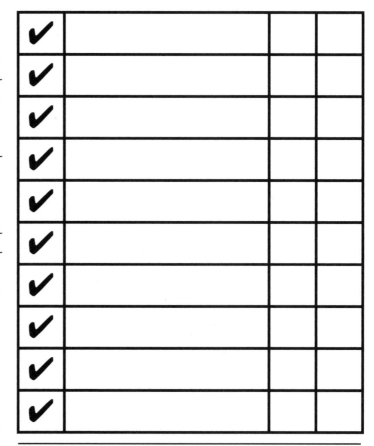

Figure 1.2. List menu.

Benefits

Responsibility. Students have complete control over their grades. They really like the idea that they can guarantee their grade if they complete their required work. If they lose points on one of the chosen assignments, they can complete another to be sure they have met their goal points.

Concept Reinforcement. This menu also allows for an in-depth study of material; however, with the different levels of Bloom's Revised taxonomy being represented, students who are still learning the concepts can choose some of the lower level point value projects to reinforce the basics before jumping into the higher level activities.

Limitations

Few Topics. This menu is best used for one topic in depth, although it can be used for up to three different topics.

Cannot Guarantee Objectives. If it is used for three topics, it is possible for a student to not have to complete an activity for each objective, depending on the choices he or she makes.

Preparation. Teachers need to have all materials ready at the beginning of the unit for students to be able to choose any of the activities on the list, which requires advanced planning.

Time Considerations

These menus usually are intended for shorter amounts of completion time—at the most, 2 weeks.

2–5–8 or 20-50-80 Menu

> "My least favorite menu is 2-5-8. You can't just do the easy ones. If you pick a 2, then you gotta do an 8, or you have to do 2 5s. I don't think you should do any more of these. No matter what you had to do one of hard ones."
>
> *—Seventh-grade student*

Description

A 2-5-8 Menu (see Figure 1.3), or 20-50-80 Menu, has two variations: one in which the activities are worth 2, 5, or 8 points, and one in which the activities are worth 20, 50, or 80. The 20, 50, and 80 version often is easier to grade with a rubric based on 5s (like the one included in this book). Both are variations on a List Menu, with a total of at least eight predetermined choices: at least two choices with a point value

Figure 1.3. 2-5-8 menu.

of 2 (20), at least four choices with a point value of 5 (50), and at least two choices with a point value of 8 (80). Choices are assigned these points based on the levels of Bloom's Revised taxonomy. Choices with a point value of two represent the *remember* and *understand* levels, choices with a point value of five represent the *apply* and *analyze* levels, and choices with a point value of eight represent the *evaluate* and *create* levels. All levels of choices carry different weights and have different expectations for completion time and effort. Students are expected to earn 10 (100) points for a 100%. Students choose what combination they would like to use to attain that point goal.

Benefits

Responsibility. With this menu, students still have complete control over their grades.

Guaranteed Activity. This menu's design also is set up in such a way that students must complete at least one activity at a higher level of Bloom's Revised taxonomy in order to reach their point goal.

Limitations

One Topic. Although it can be used for more than one topic, this menu works best with in-depth study of one topic.

No Free Choice. By nature, it also does not allow students to propose their own free choice, because point values need to be assigned based on Bloom's Revised taxonomy.

Higher Level Thinking. Students will complete only one activity at a higher level of thinking.

Time Considerations

These menus are usually intended for a shorter amount of completion time—at the most, one week.

Baseball Menu

> "There were so many choices and most of them were fun activities!"
>
> *—Sixth-grade student*

Description

This menu (see Figure 1.4) is a baseball-based variation on the List Menu, with a total of at least 20 predetermined choices: Choices are given values as singles, doubles, triples, or home runs based on Bloom's Revised taxonomy. Singles represent the *remember* and *understand* levels; doubles, the *apply* and *analyze* levels; triples, the *evaluate* level; and home runs, the *create* level. All levels of choices carry different weights and have different expectations for completion time and effort. Students are expected to earn a certain number of runs (around all four bases) for a 100%. Students choose what combination they would like to use to attain that number of runs.

Figure 1.4. Baseball menu.

Benefits

Responsibility. With this menu, students still have complete control over their own grades.

Flexibility. This menu allows for many choices at each level. Students should have no trouble finding something that catches their interest.

Theme. This menu has a fun theme that students enjoy and can be used throughout the classroom. A bulletin board can be set up with a baseball diamond, with each student having his or her own player who can move through the bases. Not only can students keep track of their own RBIs, but they can have a visual reminder of what they have completed as well.

Limitations

One Topic. This menu is best used for one topic with many objectives for in-depth study.

Preparation. With so many choices available to students, teachers should have all materials ready at the beginning of the unit for students to be able to choose any of the activities on the list. This sometimes is a consideration for space in the classroom.

One Free Choice. This menu also only has one opportunity for free choice for students, in the home run section.

Time Considerations

These menus usually are intended for a longer amount of completion time, depending on the number of runs required for a 100%. At most, these are intended for 4 or 5 weeks.

Game Show Menu

"This menu really challenged my students. If one of my students saw another student choosing a more difficult option, they wanted to choose one, too. I had very few students choose to the basic options on this menu. It was wonderful!"

—*Sixth-grade science teacher*

Description

The Game Show Menu (see Figure 1.5) is the most complex menu. It covers multiple topics or objectives with at least three predetermined choices and a free student choice for each objective. Choices are assigned points based on the levels of Bloom's Revised taxonomy. All choices carry different weights and have different expectations for completion time and effort. A point criterion is set forth that equals 100%. Students must complete at least one activity from each objective in order to reach their goal.

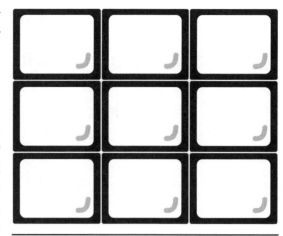

Figure 1.5. Game show menu.

Benefits

Free Choices. This menu allows many choices for students, but if they do not want to complete the offered activities, they can propose their own activity for each objective.

Responsibility. This menu allows students to guarantee their own grades.

Different Learning Levels. It has the flexibility to allow for individualized contracts for different learning levels within the classroom. Each student can create a contract for a certain number of points for his or her 100%.

Objectives Guaranteed. The teacher is guaranteed that the students complete an activity from each objective covered, even if it is at a lower level.

Limitations

Confirm Expectations. The only real limitation here is that students (and parents) must understand the guidelines for completing the menu.

Time Considerations

These menus usually are intended for a longer amount of completion time. Although they can be used as a yearlong menu (each column could be a grading period), they usually are intended for 4–6 weeks.

Free Choice

"I don't know if I really liked it at first. It's a lot easier to just do the basic stuff and get it over with but when Mrs. [teacher] told us she wanted us to submit at least one free choice, I really got into it! I mean, I could do something I wanted to do? How often do you get to do THAT in school?"

–Eighth-grade GT student

With most of the menus, the students are allowed to submit a free choice for their teacher's consideration. Figure 1.6 shows two sample proposal forms that have been used successfully in my classroom. With middle school students, this cuts down greatly on the whining that often accompanies any task given to students. A copy of these forms should be given to each student when the menu is first introduced. The form used is based on the type of menu being presented. For example, if you are using the Tic-Tac-Toe Menu, there is no need to submit a point proposal. A discussion should be held with the students so they understand the expectations of a free choice. I always have a few students who do not want to complete a task on the menu; they are welcome to create their own free choice and submit it for approval. The biggest complainers will not always go to the trouble to complete the form and have it approved, but it is their choice not to do so. The more free choice is used and encouraged, the more students will begin to request it. How the students show their knowledge will begin to shift from teacher-focused to student-designed activities. If students do not want to make a proposal using the proposal form after the teacher has discussed the entire menu and its activities, they can place the unused form in a designated place in the classroom. Others may want to use their form, and it often is surprising who wants to submit a proposal form after hearing about the opportunity!

Proposal forms must be submitted before students begin working on their free-choice products. The teacher then knows what the students are working on and the students know the expectations the teacher has for that product. Once approved, the forms easily can be stapled to the students' menu sheets. The students can refer to it as they develop their free-choice product, and when the grading takes place, the teacher can refer to the agreement for the graded features of the product.

Name: _____   Teacher's Approval: _____

Free-Choice Proposal Form for Point-Based Menu

Points Requested: _____   Points Approved: _____

<u>Proposal Outline</u>

1. What specific topic or idea will you learn about?

2. What criteria should be used to grade it? (Neatness, content, creativity, artistic value, etc.)

3. What will your product look like?

4. What materials will you need from the teacher to create this product?

Name: _____   Teacher's Approval: _____

Free-Choice Proposal Form

<u>Proposal Outline</u>

1. What specific topic or idea will you learn about?

2. What criteria should be used to grade it? (Neatness, content, creativity, artistic value, etc.)

3. What will your product look like?

4. What materials will you need from the teacher to create this product?

Figure 1.6. Sample proposal forms for free choice.

Each part of the proposal form is important and needs to be discussed with students.

- *Name/Teacher's Approval.* The student must submit this form to the teacher for approval. The teacher will carefully review all of the information, send it back to the student for correction, if needed, and then sign the top.

- *Points Requested.* Found only on the point-based menu proposal form, this usually is where negotiation needs to take place. Students usually will submit their first request for a very high number (even the 100% goal.) They equate the amount of time something will take with the amount of points it should earn. But, please note, the points are *always* based on the levels of Bloom's Revised taxonomy. For example, a PowerPoint presentation with a vocabulary word quiz would get minimal points, although it may have taken a long time to create. If the students have not been exposed to the levels of Bloom's Revised taxonomy, this can be difficult to explain. You always can refer to the popular "Bloom's Verbs" to help explain the difference between time requirements and higher level activities.

- *Points Approved.* Found only on the point-based menu proposal form, this is the final decision recorded by the teacher once the point haggling is finished.

- *Proposal Outline.* This is where the student will tell you everything about the product he or she intends to complete. These questions should be completed in such a way that you can really picture what the student is planning on completing. This also shows you that the student knows what he or she is planning on completing.

  - *What specific topic or idea will you learn about?* Students need to be specific here. It is not acceptable to write *science* or *reading*. This is where they look at the objectives of the product and choose which objective their product demonstrates.

  - *What criteria should be used to grade it?* Although there are rubrics for all of the products that the students might create, it is important for the students to explain what criteria are most important to evaluate the product. The student may indicate that the rubric being used for all of the predetermined products is fine; however, he or she also may want to add other criteria here.

  - *What will your product look like?* It is important for this to be as detailed as possible. If a student cannot express what it will "look like," he or she has probably not given the free-choice plan enough thought.

- *What materials will you need from the teacher to create this product?* This is an important consideration. Sometimes students do not have the means to purchase items for their product. This can be negotiated as well, but if you ask what students may need, they often will develop even grander ideas for their free choice.

CHAPTER 2

How to Use Menus in the Classroom

There are different ways to use instructional menus in the classroom. In order to decide how to implement each menu, the following should be considered: How much prior knowledge of the topic being taught do the students have before the unit or lesson begins, and how much information is readily available for students to obtain on their own? After considering these two questions, there are three customary ways to use menus in the classroom.

Enrichment and Supplemental Activities

Using the menus for enrichment and supplementary activities is the most common way to implement this tool. Usually, the teacher will introduce the menu and the activities at the beginning of the unit. In this case, the students usually do not have a lot of background knowledge and the information about the topic may not be readily available to all students. The teacher then will progress through the content at the normal rate using his or her curricular materials, periodically allowing class and homework time throughout the unit for students to work on their menu choices to supplement a deeper understanding of the lessons being taught. This method is very effective, as it builds in an immediate use for the content the teacher is covering. For example, at the beginning of a unit on mixtures, the teacher many introduce the menu with the explanation that students may not have all of the knowledge to complete all of their choices yet. During the unit, however, more content will be provided and the students will be prepared to work on new choices. If students want to work ahead, they certainly can find the information on their own, but that is not required. Gifted students often see this as a challenge and will begin to investigate concepts mentioned in the menu before the teacher introduces them. This helps build an immense pool of background knowledge before the topic is even discussed in the classroom. As teachers, we fight the battle of having students read ahead or "come to class prepared to discuss." By introducing a menu at the beginning of a unit and allowing students to complete products as instruction progresses, the students naturally investigate the information and come to class prepared without it being a completely separate requirement.

Standard Activities

Another option for using menus in the classroom is to replace certain curricular activities the teacher uses to teach the specified content. In this case, the students may have some limited background knowledge about the content, and information is readily available for them in their classroom resources. The teacher would pick and choose which aspects of the content must be directly taught to the students and which could be appropriately learned and reinforced through product menus. The unit then is designed using both formal instructional lessons and specific menu days where the students will use the menu to reinforce the prior knowledge they already have learned. In order for this option to be effective, the teacher must feel very comfortable with the students' prior knowledge level. Another variation on this method is using the menus to drive center or station activities. Centers have many different functions in the classroom—most importantly reinforcing the instruction that has taken place. Rather than having a set rotation for centers, the teacher could use the menu activities as enrichment or supplementary activities during center time for those students who need more than just reinforcement; centers could be set up with the materials students would need to complete various products.

Mini-Lessons

The third option for menu use is the use of mini-lessons, with the menus driving the accompanying classroom activities. This method is best used when the majority of the students have a lot of prior knowledge about the topic. The teacher would design short 10–15-minute mini-lessons, where students would quickly review or introduce basic concepts that already are familiar to them. The students then are turned loose to choose an activity on the menu to show they understand the concept. The Game Show Menu usually works very well with this method of instruction, as the topics across the top usually lend themselves very well to the mini-lessons. It is important that the students have prior knowledge on the content because the lesson cycle is cut very short in this use of menus. Using menus in this way does not allow the guided practice step of the lesson, as it is assumed the students already understand the information. The teacher simply is reviewing the information and then moving right to the higher levels of Bloom's Revised taxonomy by asking students to create a product. By using the menus in this way, the teacher avoids the "I already know this" glossy looks from his or her students. Another important consideration is the independence level of the students. In order for this use of menus to be effective, students will need to be able to work independently for up to 30 minutes after the mini-lesson. Usually because interest is high in the product they have chosen, this is not a critical issue, but still one worth mentioning as teachers consider how they would like to use various menus in their classroom. Menus can be used in many different ways; all are based on the knowledge and capabilities of the students working on them!

CHAPTER 3

Guidelines for Products

> "... I got to do a play! In math!!"
>
> —*Seventh-grade student*

This chapter outlines the different types of products included in the featured menus, as well as the guidelines and expectations for each. It is very important that students know the expectations of a completed product when they choose to work on it. By discussing these expectations *before* students begin and having the information readily available for students, you will limit frustration on everyone's part.

$1 Contract

Consideration should be given to the cost of creating the products in any menu. The resources available to students vary within a classroom, and students should not be graded on the amount of materials they can purchase to make a product look better. These menus are designed to equalize the resources students have available. The materials for most products are available for less than a dollar and often can be found in a teacher's classroom as part of the classroom supplies. If a product requires

---

$1 Contract

I did not spend more than $1.00 on my _____.

_____   _____
            Student Signature   Date

My child, _____, did not spend more than $1.00 on the product
he or she created.

_____   _____
            Parent Signature   Date

Figure 3.1. $1 contract.

materials from the student, there is a $1 contract as part of the product criteria. This is a very important piece in the explanation of the product. First of all, by limiting the amount of money a child can spend, it creates an equal amount of resources for all students. Second, it actually encourages a more creative product. When students are limited by the amount of materials they can readily purchase, they often have to use materials from home in new and unique ways. Figure 3.1 is a sample $1 contract that has been used many times in my classroom with various products.

The Products

Table 3.1 contains a list of the products used in this book. These products were chosen for their flexibility in meeting learning styles, as well as for being products many teachers already encourage in their classroom. They have been arranged by learning style—visual, kinesthetic, or auditory—and each menu has been designed to include products from all of the learning styles. Of course, some of the products may be listed in more than one area depending on how they are presented or implemented. The specific expectations for all of the products are presented in an easy-to-read card format that can be reproduced for students (see Figure 3.2).

The format is convenient for students to have in front of them when they work on their products. These cards also can be laminated and posted

Table 3.1
Products

Visual	Kinesthetic	Auditory
Acrostic	Bulletin Board Display	Children's Book
Advertisement	Class Game	Commercial/Infomercial
Book Cover	Commercial/Infomercial	Game Show
Brochure/Pamphlet	Concentration Cards	Interview
Bulletin Board Display	Cross-Cut Model	News Report
Cartoon/Comic Strip	Diorama	Oral Presentation of Created
Children's Book	Flipbook	Product
Collage	Folded Quiz Book	Play/Skit
Cross-Cut Diagram	Game	PowerPoint—Speaker
Crossword Puzzle	Mobile	Puppet
Diary/Journal	Model	Song/Rap
Drawing	Mural	Speech
Essay	Play/Skit	Student-Taught Lesson
Folded Quiz Book	Product Cube	Video
Greeting Card	Puppet	You Be the Person
Instruction Card	Quiz Board	Presentation
Letter	Science Experiment	
Map	Student-Taught Lesson	
Mind Map	Three-Dimensional Timeline	
Newspaper Article	Trophy	
Paragraph	Video	
Pie Graph		
Poster		
PowerPoint—Stand Alone		
Questionnaire		
Quiz		
Quiz Board		
Recipe/Recipe Card		
Scrapbook		
Story		
Three Facts and a Fib		
Trading Cards		
Venn Diagram		
Video		
WebQuest		
Windowpane		
Worksheet		

on a bulletin board for easy access during classroom work. Some teachers prefer to only give a few product guidelines at a time, while others will provide all of the pages so students feel comfortable venturing out in their free choices. Students enjoy looking at all of the different products and it can stimulate ideas as they peruse the guidelines.

Acrostic	Advertisement	Book Cover
• At least 8.5" by 11" • Neatly written or typed • Target word will be written down the left side of the paper • Each descriptive phrase chosen must begin with one of the letters from the target word • Each descriptive phrase chosen must be related to the target word	• At least 8.5" by 11" • A slogan should be included • Color picture of item or service • Include price, if appropriate • Can be developed on the computer	• Front cover—title, author, image • Cover inside flap—paragraph summary of the book • Back inside flap—brief biography of author with at least five details • Back cover—editorial comments about the book • Spine—title and author
Brochure/Pamphlet	**Bulletin Board Display**	**Cartoon/Comic Strip**
• At least 8.5" by 11" • Must be in three-fold format; front fold has the title and picture • Must have both pictures and written text • Information should be in paragraph form with at least five facts included • Bibliography should be provided as needed • Can be created on computer • Any pictures from Internet must have proper credit	• Must fit within assigned space on bulletin board or wall • Must include at least 10 details • Must have a title • Must have at least five different elements (posters, papers, questions, etc.) • Must have at least one interactive element that engages the reader	• At least 8.5" by 11" • At least six cells • Must have meaningful dialogue • Must include color
Children's Book	**Class Game**	**Collage**
• Must have a cover with book's title and student's name as author • Must have at least 10 pages • Each page should have an illustration to accompany the story • Should be neatly written or typed • Can be developed on the computer	• Game will allow all class members to participate • Must have only a few, easy-to-understand rules • Should be inventive or a new variation on a current game • Must have multiple question opportunities • Must provide answer key before the game is played • The game must be approved by the teacher before being scheduled for play	• At least 8.5" by 11" • Pictures must be cut neatly from magazines or newspapers (no clip art) • Label items as required in task
Commercial/Infomercial	**Concentration Cards**	**Cross-Cut Model/Diagram**
• Must be 2–4 minutes in length • Script must be turned in before commercial is presented • Can be presented live to an audience or recorded on a VHS tape or DVD • Should have props or some form of costume(s) • Can include more than one person	• At least 20 index cards (10 matching sets) must be made • Both pictures and words can be used • Information should be placed on just one side of each card • Include an answer key that shows the matches • All cards must be submitted in a carrying bag	• Must include a scale to show the relationship between the product and the actual item • Must include details about each layer • If creating a model, also must meet the criteria of a model • If creating a diagram, also must meet the criteria of a poster

Figure 3.2. Product guidelines.

Crossword Puzzle	Diary/Journal	Diorama
• At least 20 significant words or phrases should be included • Develop appropriate clues • Include puzzle and answer key • Can be created on the computer	• Neatly written or typed • Should include the appropriate number of entries • Should include a date if appropriate • Should be written in first person	• At least 4" by 5" by 8" • Must be self-standing • All interior space must be covered with relevant pictures and information • Name written on the back in permanent ink • Informational/title card attached to diorama • $1 contract signed
Drawing	**Essay**	**Flipbook**
• Must be at least 8.5" by 11" • Must show what is requested in the task statement • Must include color • Must be neatly drawn by hand • Must have title • Name should be written on the back	• Neatly written or typed • Must cover the specific topic in detail • Must be at least three paragraphs • Must include resources or bibliography if appropriate	• At least 8.5" by 11" folded in half • All information or opinions are supported by facts • Created with the correct number of flaps cut into the top • Color is optional • Name must be written on the back
Folded Quiz Book	**Game**	**Game Show**
• At least 8.5" by 11" folded in half • At least 10 questions • Created with the correct number of flaps cut into the top • Questions written or typed neatly on upper flaps • Answers written or typed neatly inside each flap • Color is optional • Name written on the back	• At least four thematic game pieces • At least 25 colored/thematic squares • At least 20 question/activity cards • Include a thematic title on the board • Include a complete set of rules for playing the game • At least the size of an open file folder	• Needs an emcee or host • Must have at least two contestants • There must be at least one regular round and a bonus round • Questions will be content specific • Props can be used, but are not mandatory
Greeting Card	**Instruction Card**	**Interview**
• Front—colored pictures, words optional • Front inside—personal note related to topic • Back inside—greeting or saying; must meet product criteria • Back outside—logo, publisher, and price for card	• No larger than 5" by 8" • Created on heavy paper or card • Neatly written or typed • Uses color drawings • Provides instructions stated in the task	• Must have at least eight questions relevant to the topic being studied • Person chosen for interview must be an "expert" and qualified to provide answers based on product criteria • Questions and answers must be neatly written or typed

Figure 3.2. Product guidelines, continued.

Letter	Map	Mind Map
• Neatly written or typed • Uses proper letter format • At least three paragraphs in length • Must follow type of letter stated in the menu (e.g., friendly, persuasive, informational)	• At least 8.5" by 11" • Accurate information is included • Includes at least 10 relevant locations • Includes compass rose, legend, scale, and key	• At least 8.5" by 11" • Uses unlined paper • Must have one central idea • Follows the "no more than four" rule—no more than four words coming from any one word • Should be neatly written or developed using Inspiration
Mobile	**Model**	**Mural**
• At least 10 pieces of related information • Includes color and pictures • At least three layers of hanging information • Hangs in a balanced way	• At least 8" by 8" by 12" • Parts of model must be labeled • Should be in scale when appropriate • Must include a title card • Name should be permanently written on model	• At least 22" x 54" • Must contain at least five pieces of important information • Must have colored pictures • Words are optional, but a title should be included • Name should be written on the back in a permanent way
News Report	**Newspaper Article**	**Paragraph**
• Must address the who, what, where, when, why, and how of the topic • Script of report turned in with project, or before if performance will be "live" • Must be either performed live or recorded on a VHS tape or DVD	• Must be informational in nature • Must follow standard newspaper format • Must include picture with caption that supports article • At least three paragraphs in length • Neatly written or typed	• Neatly written or typed • Must have topic sentence, at least 3 supporting sentences or details and a concluding sentence • Must use appropriate vocabulary and follow grammar rules
Pie Graph	**Play/Skit**	**Poster**
• Can be created neatly by hand or using computer software • Must have a title • Must have a label for each area or be color coded with a key • Must include the percentages for each area of the graph • Calculations must provided if needed to create the pie graph	• Must be between 5–10 minutes long • Script must be turned in before play is presented • May be presented to an audience or recorded for future showing • Should have props or some form of costume • Can include more than one person	• Should be the size of a standard poster board • Includes at least five pieces of important information • Must have title • Must contain both words and pictures • Name should be written on the back • Bibliography should be included as needed

Figure 3.2. Product guidelines, continued.

PowerPoint—Speaker	PowerPoint—Stand Alone	Product Cube
• At least 10 informational slides and one title slide with student's name • No more than two words per page • Slides must have color and no more than one graphic per page • Animations are optional but should not distract from information being presented • Presentation should be timed and flow with the speech being given	• At least 10 informational slides and one title slide with student's name • No more than 10 words per page • Slides must have color and no more than one graphic per page • Animation is optional, and must not distract from information being presented	• All six sides of the cube must be filled with information • Should be neatly written or typed • Name must be printed neatly on the bottom of one of the sides • Should be submitted flat for grading
Puppet	**Questionnaire**	**Quiz**
• Puppet should be handmade and must have a moveable mouth • A list of supplies used to make the puppet will be turned in with the puppet • $1 contract signed • If used in a play, all play criteria must be met as well	• Neatly written or typed • At least 10 questions with possible answers, and at least one answer that requires a written response • Questions must be helpful to gathering information on the topic being studied • At least 15 people must provide answers to questionnaire	• Must be at least half sheet of paper • Neatly written or typed • Must cover the specific topic in detail • Must include at least five questions including a short answer question • Must have at least one graphic • An answer key will be turned in with the quiz
Quiz Board	**Recipe/Recipe Card**	**Scrapbook**
• At least five questions • Must have at least five answers • Should use a system with lights to facilitate self-checking • Should be no larger than a poster board • Holiday lights can be used • $1 contract signed	• Must be written neatly or typed on a piece of paper or an index card • Must have a list of ingredients with measurement for each • Must have numbered steps that explain how to make the recipe	• Cover of scrapbook must have a meaningful title and student's name • Must have at least five themed pages • Each page will have at least one meaningful picture • All photos must have captions
Song/Rap	**Speech**	**Story**
• Words must make sense • Can be presented to an audience or taped • Written words will be turned in before performance or with taped song • Should be at least 2 minutes in length	• Must be at least 2 minutes in length • Should not be read from written paper • Note cards can be used • Written speech must be turned in before speech is presented • Voice must be clear, loud, and easy to understand	• Must have all of the elements of a well-written story (setting, characters, conflict, rising action, and resolution) • Must be appropriate length to allow for story elements • Should be neatly written or typed

Figure 3.2. Product guidelines, continued.

Three-Dimensional Timeline	Three Facts and a Fib	Trading Cards
• Must be no bigger than standard-size poster board • Must be divided into equal time units • Must contain at least 10 important dates and have at least 2 sentences explaining why each date is important • Must have a meaningful, creative object securely attached beside each date to represent that date • Must be able to explain how each object represents each date	• Can be written, typed, or created using Microsoft PowerPoint • Must include exactly four statements: three true statements and one false statement • False statement should not obvious • Brief paragraph should be included that explains why the fib is false	• Include at least 10 cards • Each card should be at least 3" by 5" • Each should have a colored picture • Includes at least three facts on the subject of the card • Cards must have information on both sides • All cards must be submitted in a carrying bag
Trophy	**Venn Diagram**	**Video**
• Must be at least 6 inches tall • Must have a base with the name of the recipient and the name of the award written neatly or typed on it • Top of trophy must be appropriate and represent the nature of the award • Name should be written on the bottom of the award • Must be an originally designed trophy (avoid reusing a trophy from home)	• At least 8.5" by 11" • Shapes should be thematic and neatly drawn • Must have a title for entire diagram and a title for each section • Must have at least six items in each section of the diagram • Name must be written neatly on the back of the paper	• Use VHS, DVD, or Flash format • Turn in a written plan or story board with project • Students will need to arrange their own video recorder or allow teacher at least 3 days notice for use of video recorder • Covers pertinent information about the project • Name must be written on video label
WebQuest	**Windowpane**	**Worksheet**
• Must quest through at least five high-quality Web sites • Web sites should be linked in the document • Can be submitted in a Word or PowerPoint document • At least three questions for each Web site • Must address the topic	• At least 8.5" by 11" unlined paper • At least six squares • Each square must include both a picture and words that should be neatly written or typed • All pictures should be both creative and meaningful • Name should be recorded on the bottom righthand corner of the front of the windowpane	• Must be 8.5" by 11" • Neatly written or typed • Must cover the specific topic or question in detail • Must be creative in design • Must have at least one graphic • An answer key will be turned in with the worksheet
You Be the Person Presentation		
• Take on the role of the person • Cover at least five important facts about the life of the person • Should be between 3 and 5 minutes in length • Script must be turned in before information is presented • Should be presented to an audience with the ability to answer questions while in character • Must have props or some form of costume		

Figure 3.2. Product guidelines, continued.

CHAPTER 4

Rubrics

"I frequently end up with more papers and products to grade than with a unit taught in the traditional way. Luckily, the rubric speeds up the process."

–Eighth-grade teacher

The most common reason teachers feel uncomfortable with menus is the need for equal grading. Teachers often feel it is easier to grade the same type of product made by all of the students, rather than grading a large number of different products, none of which looks like any other. The great equalizer for hundreds of different products is a generic rubric that can cover all of the important qualities of an excellent product.

All-Purpose Rubric

Figure 4.1 is an example of a rubric that has been classroom tested with various menus. This rubric can be used with any point value activity presented in a menu. When a menu is presented to students, this rubric can be reproduced on the back of the menu with its guidelines. It also can be given to students to keep in their folder with their product cards so they always know the expectations as they complete products throughout the school year. The first time students see this rubric, it should be explained in detail, especially the last column, Self. It is very important that students self-evaluate their products. This column can provide a unique perspective of the product as it is being graded. *Note*: This rubric was designed to be specific enough that students will know the criteria the teacher is seeking, but general enough that they can still be as creative as they like in the creation of their product. Because all of the point-based menus depend on points that are multiples of 5, the rubric itself has been divided into five areas to make it easier to be more objective with grading.

Student-Taught Lessons and Science Experiment Rubrics

Although the generic rubric can be used for all activities, there are two occasions that seem to warrant a special rubric: student-taught lessons and science experiments. These are unique situations, with many fine details that must be considered separately.

By middle school, most students have an understanding of the scientific method and are ready to begin their own investigations. Understanding the scientific method, however, does not always guarantee that students know how to apply it to their own investigations. The science experiment rubric (see Figure 4.2) will guide students as they develop their own.

Student-taught lessons can cause stress for both students and teachers. Teachers often would like to allow students to teach their fellow classmates, but are not comfortable with the grading aspect of the assignment. Rarely do students understand all of the components that go into designing an effective lesson. This student-taught lesson rubric (see Figure 4.3) helps focus the student on the important aspects of a well-designed lesson and allows teachers to make the evaluation a little more subjective.

All-Purpose Product Rubric

Name: _____

Criteria	Excellent (Full Credit)	Good (Half Credit)	Poor (No Credit)	Self
Content: Is the content of the product well chosen?	Content chosen represents the best choice for the product. Graphics are well chosen and related to content.	Information or graphics are related to content, but are not the best choice for the product.	Information or graphics presented do not appear to be related to topic or task.	
Completeness: Is everything included in the product?	All information needed is included. Product meets the product criteria and the criteria of the task as stated.	Some important information is missing. Product meets the product criteria and the criteria of the task as stated.	Most important information is missing. The product does not meet the task or does not meet the product criteria.	
Creativity: Is the product original?	Presentation of information is from a new perspective. Graphics are original. Product includes an element of fun and interest.	Presentation of information is from a new perspective. Graphics are not original. Product has elements of fun and interest.	There is no evidence of new thoughts or perspectives in the product.	
Correctness: Is all of the information included correct?	All information presented in the product is correct and accurate.	N/A	Any portion of the information presented in the product is incorrect.	
Communication: Is the information in the product well communicated?	All information is neat and easy to read. Product is in appropriate format and shows significant effort. Oral presentations are easy to understand and presented with fluency.	Most of the product is neat and easy to read. Product is in appropriate format and shows significant effort. Oral presentations are easy to understand, with some fluency.	The product is not neat and easy to read or the product is not in the appropriate format. It does not show significant effort. Oral presentation was not fluent or easy to understand.	
			Total Grade:	

Figure 4.1. All-purpose product rubric.

Science Experiment Rubric   Name: _____

Criteria	Excellent	Good	Fair	Poor	Self
Title: The title is appropriate: represents lab.	**5** Title is appropriate, unique, and represents lab.	**3** Title is present and appropriate, but not unique.	**1** Title is present, but there is no significance to specific lab.	**0** Not present.	
Problem/Purpose: Problem stated as question, appropriate for lab. Purpose stated as sentence.	**5** Problem/purpose is present, and contains proper punctuation and format.	**3** Problem/purpose is present and contains proper punctuation, but not proper format.	**1** Problem/purpose is present, but does not contain proper format or punctuation.	**0** Not present.	
Hypothesis: Stated as an if/then statement and relates to problem.	**10** Hypothesis is present, contains proper punctuation and format, and relates to problem.	**5** Hypothesis is present, contains proper punctuation, and relates to problem, but not in proper format.	**3** Hypothesis is present, but no obvious relation to problem. Proper punctuation, but not proper format.	**0** Not present or does not relate to problem.	
Materials: All materials present and all exact in description (e.g., "250 ml beaker" rather than "beaker").	**10** All materials present and exact in description.	**5** Missing no more than one material and all exact descriptions.	**3** Missing no more than one material and 90% of the descriptions are exact.	**0** Missing no more than one material but less than 90% of the descriptions are exact, or materials are not present.	
Procedure: Procedure is sequential and easy to read. Exact, written in a way that would allow others to repeat the experiment.	**20** The procedure is sequential, easy to read, and contains proper punctuation. The procedure is exact.	**15** The procedure is sequential and easy to read, but missing some proper punctuation. The procedure is exact.	**8** The procedure is not sequential, not easy to read, or missing some proper punctuation, but is exact.	**0** The procedure is not exact, not easy to read, not sequential, or not present.	
Data Table: Data are recorded in an appropriate manner, are easy to read and understand, and have proper units, titles, and descriptions.	**15** Data are easy to read, all numbers are entered with units, data table has title, and columns and rows are labeled.	**10** Data table has no title, but is easy to read; all numbers are entered with units; and columns and rows are labeled.	**5** Data table has no title, but is easy to read; no more than 3 numbers are entered without units; and columns and rows are labeled.	**0** Data table has no title, is not easy to read, some numbers are entered with no units, columns and rows are not labeled, or data not present.	
Representation of Data: Data are recorded in an appropriate manner, and are easy to read and understand. Graph has proper units, titles, and descriptions, and the proper graph has been chosen.	**15** Data are easy to read; graph has title, units, and descriptors; and variables are on the correct axis. Data are clearly represented.	**10** Data are easy to read; graph has units and descriptors, but no title; and variables are on the correct axis. Data are clearly represented.	**5** Data are easy to read; graph has descriptors, but no units or title; and variables are on the correct axis. Data are clearly represented.	**0** Data are easy to read, graph has missing descriptors, variables are on the incorrect axis, or not present.	
Conclusion: Conclusion is in paragraph form, revisits hypothesis, explains how the lab was conducted, suggests margins of error, and makes a new hypothesis if needed.	**20** Contains proper punctuation and form, describes experiment and points of error, and revisits hypothesis and suggests a new one if necessary.	**12** Contains proper punctuation and form, describes experiment, revisits hypothesis and suggest a new one if necessary, but does not describe points of error.	**4** Missing proper punctuation or form, or revisits hypothesis but does not suggest a new one if necessary.	**0** Does not revisit hypothesis or conclusion is not present.	
				Total Grade:	

Figure 4.2. Science experiment rubric.

Student-Taught Lesson Grading Rubric

Name: _____

Parts of Lesson	Excellent	Good	Fair	Poor	Self
Prepared and Ready: All materials and lesson ready at start of class period, from warm-up to conclusion of lesson.	**10** Everything is ready to present.	**6** Lesson is present, but small amount of scrambling.	**3** Lesson is present, but major scrambling.	**0** No lesson ready or missing major components.	
Understanding: Presenters understand the material well. Students understand information presented.	**20** All information is correct and in correct format.	**12** Presenter understands; 25% of students do not.	**4** Presenter understands; 50% of students do not.	**0** Presenter is confused.	
Complete: Includes all significant information from section or topic.	**15** Includes all important information.	**10** Includes most important information.	**2** Includes less than 50% of the important information.	**0** Information is not related.	
Practice: Includes some way for students to practice or access the information.	**20** Practice present; well chosen.	**10** Practice present; can be applied effectively.	**5** Practice present; not related or best choice.	**0** No practice or students are confused.	
Interest/Fun: Most of the class was involved, interested, and participating.	**15** Everyone interested and participating.	**10** 75% actively participating.	**5** Less than 50% actively participating.	**0** Everyone off task.	
Creativity: Information presented in an imaginative way.	**20** Wow, creative! I never would have thought of that!	**12** Good ideas!	**5** Some good pieces but general instruction.	**0** No creativity; all lecture, notes, or worksheet.	
				Total Grade:	

Your Topic/Objective:

Comments:

Don't Forget:
All copy requests and material requests must be made at least 24 hours in advance.

Figure 4.3. Student-taught lesson grading rubric.

Part 2
The Menus

How to Use the Menu Pages

Each menu in this section has:
- an introduction page for the teacher,
- the content menu,
- any specific guidelines, and
- specific activities mentioned in the menu.

Introduction Pages

The introduction pages are meant to provide an overview of each menu. They are divided into five areas.

1. *Objectives Covered Through the Menu and Activities.* This area will list all of the objectives that the menu can address. Menus are arranged in such a way that if students complete the guidelines set forth in the instructions for the menu, all of these objectives will be covered.

2. *Materials Needed by Students for Completion.* For each menu, it is expected that the teacher will provide, or students will have access to, the following materials: lined paper; glue; crayons, colored pencils, or

markers; and blank 8 ½" by 11" white paper. The introduction page also includes a list of additional materials that may be needed by students. Students do have the choice of which menu items they would like to complete, so it is possible that the teacher will not need all of these materials for every student. Some menu options may involve students developing their own experiment. This will be noted here, as well, with materials commonly used by students in their own experiments.

3. *Special Notes.* Some menus have special management issues or consideration. This section will share any tips to consider for a specific activity or product.

4. *Time Frame.* Each menu has its own ideal time frame based on its structure, but all work best with at least a one-week time frame. Menus that assess more objectives are better suited to more than 2 weeks. This section will give you an overview about the best time frame for completing the entire menu, as well as options for shorter time periods. If teachers do not have time to devote to an entire menu, they certainly can choose the 1–2-day option for any menu topic students are currently studying.

5. *Suggested Forms.* This is a list of the rubrics that should be available for students as the menus are introduced. If a menu has a free-choice option, the appropriate proposal form also will be listed here.

CHAPTER 5

Process Skills

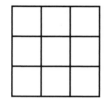

Safety and Equipment

Tic-Tac-Toe Menu

Objectives Covered Through This Menu and These Activities
- Students will state the importance of different safety rules.
- Students will identify scientific equipment and their uses.

Materials Needed by Students for Completion
- Poster board or large white paper
- Materials for board games (folders, colored cards, etc.)
- Microsoft PowerPoint or other slideshow software
- Blank index cards (for concentration game and mobile)
- Coat hangers (for mobile)
- DVD or VHS recorder
- String (for mobile)

Special Notes on the Use of This Menu
This menu gives students the opportunity to create an infomercial. Although students enjoy producing their own videos, there often are difficulties obtaining the equipment and scheduling the use of the video recorder. This can be modified by allowing students to act out the infomercial (like a play) or, if students have the technology, they may wish to produce a Webcam or Flash version of their infomercial.

Time Frame
- 2–3 weeks—Students are given the menu as the unit is started. As the teacher presents lessons throughout the week, he or she should refer back to the menu options associated with that content. The teacher will go over all of the options for that content and have students place checkmarks in the boxes that represent the activities they are most interested in completing. As teaching continues over the next 2–3 weeks, activities chosen and completed should make a column or row. When students complete this pattern, they have completed one activity from each content area, learning style, or level of Bloom's, depending on the design of the menu.
- 1 week—At the start of the unit, the teacher chooses the three activities he or she feels are most valuable for the students. Stations can be set up in the classroom. These three activities are available for student choice throughout the week as regular instruction takes place.

- 1–2 days—The teacher chooses an activity from the menu to use with the entire class.

Suggested Forms
- All-purpose rubric
- Free-choice proposal form

Safety and Equipment

☐ *Equipment Mobile* There are different ways to sort or group the equipment used in the science lab. Create a mobile that shows how the equipment can be sorted. Include drawings for each.	☐ *Safety Poster* Design a poster that illustrates the most important safety rule. The poster should be appropriate for a fourth grader or younger. Instead of stating the rule in sentence form, show it using pictures.	☐ *Dr. Beaker's Infomercial* Dr. Beaker, the science safety guru, has decided to create a video on using equipment safely for middle school students. Create your own version of Dr. Beaker's video.
☐ *Dr. Beaker's Safety Quiz* Dr. Beaker, the accident-prone scientist, has been given the task to create a safety quiz worksheet to test how to use equipment safely. Create Dr. Beaker's worksheet quiz and have one of your classmates take it.	☐ *Free Choice: Equipment* (Fill out your proposal form before beginning the free choice!)	☐ *Prove With Evidence* Look through all of the rules given. Decide which rule you feel is the most important of all. Develop a plan to prove that this rule is the most important! Be sure to include examples and evidence as to why this rule was chosen.
☐ *Safety Role-Play* Choose one your safety rules and develop a skit that shows how to follow (or not follow) this rule. Be ready to perform for the class!	☐ *Dr. Beaker Makes the News!* A local news reporter has been sent to interview Dr. Beaker, a local scientist who has the record for the most lab accidents in one year. Write a newspaper article that documents all of his accidents and how they could have been prevented.	☐ *Equipment Game* Create a concentration game that includes pictures of various pieces of equipment and their uses.

Check the boxes you plan to complete. They should form a tic-tac-toe across or down.
All products are due by: _____.

Metrics and Measurement

Tic-Tac-Toe Menu

Objectives Covered Through This Menu and These Activities

- Students will identify metric prefixes and their meaning.
- Students will explain how to convert between metric measurements.
- Students will understand the benefits of using the metric system.
- Students will become more proficient in metric estimation.

Materials Needed by Students for Completion

- Poster board or large white paper
- Graph paper or Internet access
- Blank index cards (for card game and instruction cards)

Time Frame

- 2–3 weeks—Students are given the menu as the unit is started. As the teacher presents lessons throughout the week, he or she should refer back to the menu options associated with that content. The teacher will go over all of the options for that content and have students place checkmarks in the boxes that represent the activities they are most interested in completing. As teaching continues over the next 2–3 weeks, activities chosen and completed should make a column or row. When students complete this pattern, they have completed one activity from each content area, learning style, or level of Bloom's, depending on the design of the menu.
- 1 week—At the start of the unit, the teacher chooses the three activities he or she feels are most valuable for the students. Stations can be set up in the classroom. These three activities are available for student choice throughout the week as regular instruction takes place.
- 1–2 days—The teacher chooses an activity from the menu to use with the entire class.

Suggested Forms

- Lab report rubric
- All-purpose rubric
- Student-taught lesson rubric
- Free-choice proposal form

Name:_____ Date:_____

Metrics and Measurement

☐ *Converting Metric Units* Design a how-to brochure that explains the various prefixes and how to convert between the units of measurement.	☐ *Metrics and Measurement* Create a class lesson on metrics and measurement. It should include an activity that allows your classmates to practice their metric estimation and measurement skills.	☐ *Using Metrics* Many countries use metric as their system of measurement. The United States is an exception. Should the U.S. change to only metrics? Research both systems and defend your answer in a product of your choice.
☐ *Using Metrics* Create a card game that will help its players remember the metric units with examples and their prefixes and what they mean.	☐ **Free Choice: Converting Metric Units** (Fill out your proposal form before beginning the free choice!)	☒ *Metrics and Measurement* Create an instruction card on how to estimate metric measurements using household objects. Use creative objects!
☒ *Metrics and Measurement* Make a list of 15 items in the classroom: 5 measured in grams, 5 measured in liters, and 5 measured in meters. Develop a data table to record your predictions for each of these measurements, and then measure them. Calculate your percentage error.	☒ *Using Metrics* One of the few measurements that has not become metric is time. Consider the impact of basing our time on 10. Write a newspaper article about the impact of a metric time system on our present lives.	☐ *Converting Metric Units* Make a worksheet to practice metric conversions. Include all of the prefixes and units.

Check the boxes you plan to complete. They should form a tic-tac-toe across or down.
All products are due by: _____.

Scientific Processes

Game Show Menu

Objectives Covered Through This Menu and These Activities

- Students will brainstorm and identify testable questions.
- Students will distinguish testable from not testable questions.
- Students will understand the importance of background research as part of the scientific process.
- Students will differentiate between observations and inferences.
- Students will understand the limitations of inferences.
- Students will show data in different ways.
- Students will understand that data can be shown in biased ways.
- Students will draw conclusions based on observations.

Materials Needed by Students for Completion

- Poster board or large white paper
- Blank index cards (for recipe cards)
- Materials for science experiment
- Product cube template
- Microsoft PowerPoint or other slideshow software

Time Frame

- 2–3 weeks—Students are given the menu as the unit is started and the guidelines and point expectations on the back of the menu are discussed. As lessons are taught throughout the unit, students and the teacher can refer back to the options associated with that topic. The teacher will go over all of the options for the topic being covered and have students place checkmarks in the boxes next to the activities they are most interested in completing. As teaching continues throughout the 2–3 weeks, activities are discussed, chosen, and submitted for grading.
- 1 week—At the beginning of the unit, the teacher chooses an activity from each area that he or she feels would be most valuable for students. Stations can be set up in the classroom. These activities are available for student choice throughout the week as regular instruction takes place.
- 1–2 days—The teacher chooses an activity from an objective to use with the entire class during that lesson time.

Suggested Forms
- Lab report rubric
- All-purpose rubric
- Student-taught lesson rubric
- Free-choice proposal form for point-based products

Guidelines for the Scientific Processes Game Show Menu

- You must choose at least one activity from each topic area.

- You may not do more than two activities in any one topic area for credit. (You are, of course, welcome to do more than two for your own investigation.)

- Grading will be ongoing, so turn in products as you complete them.

- All free-choice proposals must be turned in and approved *prior* to working on that free choice.

- You must earn 120 points for a 100%. You may earn extra credit up to _____ points.

- You must show your teacher your plan for completion by: _____.

Scientific Processes

Testable Questions	Background Research	Observations and Inferences	Recording and Presenting Data	Drawing Conclusions	Points for Each Level
☒ Make a two-column list that shows at least 10 examples of testable and nontestable questions. For each nontestable question, include a brief statement about why it is not testable. (15 pts.)	☒ Create a cube with six questions you can use to help conduct background research before experimenting. (15 pts.)	☒ Choose an object in your classroom. Record at least 10 observations, both qualitative and quantitative, about your object. Also record at least five inferences about your object. (10 pts.)	☒ Create a PowerPoint presentation that shows the various ways data can be recorded as well as shown through graphs and tables. (15 pts.)	☒ Create a worksheet to help your classmates practice drawing conclusions. (15 pts.)	10–15 points
☒ Create a recipe card that explains what is necessary for a question to be considered testable. (20 pts.)	☐ In order to obtain background knowledge on experiments, create a list of questions and sources your classmates could consult. (20 pts.)	☒ Read the fable "The Blind Men and the Elephant." This fable exemplifies the importance of observations and inferences. Create your own fable with the same moral. (25 pts.)	☒ Create a questionnaire to survey your classmates on a topic of your choice. After choosing the best method to show your data, create a poster to share your results. (20 pts.)	☐ Research the various theories of spontaneous generation that were shared before Francesco Redi's experiment. Create a cartoon for the conclusion you find most interesting. (25 pts.)	20–25 points
☐ Brainstorm a testable question and create a scientific experiment that answers your question. (30 pts.)	☒ Create a brochure about the benefits of doing background research before beginning an experiment. (30 pts.)	☐ Lateral thinking puzzles use both observations and inferences to solve them. Research examples of these puzzles and create two examples of your own. (30 pts.)	☐ Researchers have said that data can be biased and made to look like they support any viewpoint. Research this and create your own example of bias in presenting data. (30 pts.)	☒ Most scientists believe experiments require at least three trials to prove their observations are correct. Create a humorous play that shows the importance of multiple trials. (30 pts.)	30 points
Free Choice (prior approval) (25–50 pts.)	**Free Choice** (prior approval) (25–50 pts.)	**Free Choice** (prior approval) (25–50 pts.)	**Free Choice** (prior approval) (25–50 pts.)	**Free Choice** (prior approval) (25–50 pts.)	25–50 points
Total:	**Total:**	**Total:**	**Total:**	**Total:**	**Total Grade:**

Background Research Cube

Complete a cube to help conduct background research. Each side of the cube should have a probing question that would help its user conduct effective background research. Use this pattern or create your own cube.

© Prufrock Press Inc. • *Differentiating Instruction With Menus: Middle School Edition: Science*

This page may be photocopied or reproduced with permission for student use.

51

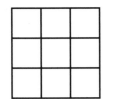

Famous Scientists

Tic-Tac-Toe Menu

Objectives Covered Through This Menu and These Activities
- Students will research scientists important to the current unit of study.
- Students will investigate why scientists are famous.

Materials Needed by Students for Completion
- Poster board or large white paper
- Graph paper or Internet access
- Microsoft PowerPoint or other slideshow software
- Scrapbooking materials
- Magazines (for collage)
- Materials for three-dimensional timeline

Time Frame
- 2–3 weeks—Students are given the menu as the unit is started. As the teacher presents lessons throughout the week, he or she should refer back to the menu options associated with that content. The teacher will go over all of the options for that content and have students place checkmarks in the boxes that represent the activities they are most interested in completing. As teaching continues over the next 2–3 weeks, activities chosen and completed should make a column or row. When students complete this pattern, they have completed one activity from each content area, learning style, or level of Bloom's, depending on the design of the menu.
- 1 week—At the start of the unit, the teacher chooses the three activities he or she feels are most valuable for the students. Stations can be set up in the classroom. These three activities are available for student choice throughout the week as regular instruction takes place.
- 1–2 days—The teacher chooses an activity from the menu to use with the entire class.

Suggested Forms
- All-purpose rubric
- Free-choice proposal form

Name:_____ Date:_____

Famous Scientists

☐ *Prepare a Speech* A scientist from our current unit of study is receiving a lifetime achievement award. The scientist has been asked to share his or her impact on history. Design a trophy and prepare the scientist's acceptance speech.	☐ *Create a PowerPoint Presentation* Choose one significant scientist from our current unit of study. Create a PowerPoint presentation to accompany a speech on your chosen scientist and his or her significant contributions to science.	☐ *Design a Greeting Card* After hearing about the scientific contributions made by scientists from our current unit of study, a greeting card company has decided to create a special line of "congratulations on your work" greeting cards. Create a greeting card that one of the scientists would appreciate.
☐ *Create a Scrapbook* Choose one scientist from our current unit of study that most interests you. Create a scrapbook about this scientist's life and accomplishments including how his or her work has impacted present day.	☐ *Free Choice: Famous Scientists* (Fill out your proposal form before beginning the free choice!)	☐ *Make a Timeline* Choose one scientist from our current unit of study and create a three-dimensional timeline of his or her life and contributions. At least two of the dates should be after the scientist's death if the person is no longer living.
☐ *Design a Book Cover* There is a new biography being written about a well-known scientist from our current unit. Design a book cover for this scientist's biography.	☐ *You Be the Star!* Research one scientist from our current unit of study. Prepare a "You Be the Person" presentation for the class.	☐ *Write a Newspaper Article* You have been asked to interview a famous scientist from our current unit of study. Develop appropriate interview questions, locate the answers, and write a newspaper article with the information about the scientist and his or her impact on history.

Check the boxes you plan to complete. They should form a tic-tac-toe across or down.
All products are due by: _____.

CHAPTER 6

Physical Sciences

Matter

Tic-Tac-Toe Menu

Objectives Covered Through This Menu and These Activities

- Students will discuss the contributions of scientists who have worked on atomic structure.
- Students will distinguish between atoms, elements, and compounds.
- Students will express the location and importance of the particles found in an atom.

Materials Needed by Students for Completion

- Materials to create models for atoms, elements, and compounds
- Poster board or large white paper
- Scrapbooking materials
- Magazines (for collage)
- Materials for three-dimensional timeline

Time Frame

- 2–3 weeks—Students are given the menu as the unit is started. As the teacher presents lessons throughout the week, he or she should refer back to the menu options associated with that content. The teacher will go over all of the options for that content and have students place checkmarks in the boxes that represent the activities they are most interested in completing. As teaching continues over the next 2–3 weeks, activities chosen and completed should make a column or row. When students complete this pattern, they have completed one activity from each content area, learning style, or level of Bloom's, depending on the design of the menu.
- 1 week—At the start of the unit, the teacher chooses the three activities he or she feels are most valuable for the students. Stations can be set up in the classroom. These three activities are available for student choice throughout the week as regular instruction takes place.
- 1–2 days—The teacher chooses an activity from the menu to use with the entire class.

Suggested Forms

- All-purpose rubric
- Free-choice proposal form

Name:_____ Date:_____

Matter

☐ *Structure of the Atom* Create a worksheet for your classmates that helps them review the structure of the atom.	☐ *History of the Atom* Research the contributions of the various scientists who have influenced how we view the structure of the atom. Choose the one who had the greatest impact on history and create a "You Be the Person" presentation for the class.	☐ *Atoms, Elements, and Compounds* Create a model out of household objects that shows the relationship between atoms, elements, and compounds.
☐ *Atoms, Elements, and Compounds* Design a folded quiz book that discusses the properties of atoms, elements, and compounds.	☐ **Free Choice: Structure of the Atom** (Fill out your proposal form before beginning the free choice!)	☐ *History of the Atom* Create a scrapbook for the history of an atom of your choice. It should document the work of key scientists, and how each contributed to change and develop the present view of atomic structure.
☐ *History of the Atom* Design a three-dimensional timeline that shows how our knowledge about the structure of the atom has changed since the time of the ancient Greeks.	☐ *Atoms, Elements, and Compounds* Create a collage with at least 10 examples of elements and compounds that we find in our daily lives.	☐ *Structure of the Atom* Write a children's book that would help younger students understand the particles found in an atom and the roles they play. Be creative!

Check the boxes you plan to complete. They should form a tic-tac-toe across or down.

All products are due by: _____.

Periodic Table Challenge

List Menu

Objectives Covered Through This Menu and These Activities
- Students will explain how the periodic table has changed over time.
- Students will understand the arrangement of the periodic table.
- Students will state the properties of families found on the periodic table.
- Students will understand the relationship between the element symbol and its name.

Materials Needed by Students for Completion
- Poster board or large white paper
- Graph paper or Internet access (for crossword puzzle)
- Ruler (for comic strip)
- Coat hangers (for mobile)
- Index cards (for mobile and trading cards)
- Large lined index cards (for instruction card)
- String (for mobile)
- Materials for board games (folders, colored cards, etc.)
- Scrapbooking materials
- Internet access (for WebQuest)

Special Notes on the Use of This Menu
This menu allows students to create a WebQuest. There are multiple versions and templates for WebQuests available on the Internet. Teachers should decide whether to specify a certain format or allow students to create one of their own choosing.

Time Frame
- 1–2 weeks—Students are given the menu as the unit is started and the guidelines and point expectations are discussed. Students usually will need to earn 100 points for 100%, although there is an opportunity for extra credit if the teacher would like to use another target number. Because this menu covers one topic in depth, the teacher will go over all of the options on the menu and have students place checkmarks in the boxes next to the activities they are most interested in completing. Teachers will need to set aside a few moments with each student to

sign the agreement at the bottom of the page. As instruction continues, activities are completed by students and submitted for grading.

- 1–2 days—The teacher chooses an activity or product from an objective to use with the entire class during that lesson time.

Suggested Forms

- All-purpose rubric
- Free-choice proposal form for point-based products

Name:_____ Date:_____

Periodic Table Challenge

Guidelines:
1. You may complete as many of the activities listed within the time period.
2. You may choose any combination of activities.
3. Your goal is 100 points. You may earn up to _____ points extra credit.
4. You may be as creative as you like within the guidelines listed below.
5. You must show your plan to your teacher by _____.
6. Activities may be turned in at any time during the working time period. They will be graded and recorded on this sheet as you continue to work, so keep it safe!

Plan to Do	Activity to Complete	Point Value	Date Completed	Points Earned
	Make a crossword puzzle with at least 20 significant vocabulary words about the periodic table.	25		
	Complete another student's crossword puzzle.	10		
	Draw a comic strip that shows how the periodic table has changed over time. (Be sure to include significant scientists!)	25		
	Make a mobile showing the families of the periodic table and three properties for each.	20		
	Make a periodic table board game.	30		
	Explain in a 1–2 page essay how you think the periodic table could change in the next 50 years. Include a drawing of how it might be different.	25		
	Choose five elements whose symbols do not directly match their element's name. Create a set of five trading cards for these elements that includes why their symbols are obvious.	20		
	Create a song or rap to help you remember the families and their properties.	25		
	Create a product of your choice that shows the families of the periodic table and at least five characteristics of each.	20		
	Choose your favorite family in the periodic table and create a family scrapbook. Include properties of the family as well as individual elements.	20		
	Create a WebQuest for the history and arrangement of the periodic table.	30		
	Complete another student's WebQuest.	10		
	Create Three Facts and a Fib for the arrangement of the periodic table.	20		
	You have been given an unknown element. Create an instruction card that would explain how to determine its family.	25		
	Write a children's book about the periodic table and its families.	30		
	Submit a free-choice proposal form for a product of your choice.	10–30		
	Total number of points you are planning to earn.	**Total points earned:**		

I am planning to complete _____ activities that could earn up to a total of _____ points.

Teacher's initials _____ Student's signature _____

Mixtures

20-50-80 Menu

Objectives Covered Through This Menu and These Activities

- Students will distinguish the physical properties of a mixture.
- Students will understand the difference between a mixture and a compound.

Materials Needed by Students for Completion

- Poster board or large white paper
- Coat hangers (for mobile)
- Index cards (for mobile)
- String (for mobile)
- Microsoft PowerPoint or other slideshow software
- Graph paper or Internet access (for crossword puzzle)
- Product cube template
- DVD or VHS recorder

Special Notes on the Use of This Menu

This menu gives students the opportunity to create an infomercial. Although students enjoy producing their own videos, there often are difficulties obtaining the equipment and scheduling the use of the video recorder. This can be modified by allowing students to act out the infomercial (like a play) or, if students have the technology, they may wish to produce a Webcam or Flash version of their infomercial.

Time Frame

- 1–2 weeks—Students are given the menu as the unit is started, and the teacher discusses all of the product options on the menu. As the different options are discussed, students will choose products that add to a total of 100 points. As the lessons progress through the week(s), the teacher and students refer back to the menu options associated with content being taught.
- 1–2 days—The teacher chooses an activity or product from the menu to use with the entire class.

Suggested Forms

- All-purpose rubric
- Free-choice proposal form for point-based products

Name:_____ Date:_____

Mixtures

Directions: Choose two activities from the menu below. The activities must total 100 points. Place a checkmark next to each box to show which activities you will complete. All activities must be completed by _____.

---

20 Points

❒ Create a worksheet for mixtures that focuses on their properties, their identification, and what makes them different from compounds.

❒ Create a mobile for the different types of mixtures with examples of each.

---

50 Points

❒ Gold jewelry is not made from pure gold; instead, it is a mixture. Prepare a PowerPoint presentation that shares how different gold mixtures are created and why they are necessary.

❒ Write a song or rap that tells how to distinguish a mixture from a compound.

❒ Create a crossword puzzle in which the clues are properties of everyday mixtures.

❒ Make a cube to assist other students who may be rolling the cube in identifying whether their substance is a mixture or a compound.

---

80 Points

❒ Think about all of the mixtures you encounter on a daily basis. Not counting air or tap water, consider which is most important to you. Create an informational video that shares the properties of your chosen mixture and its importance.

❒ Many occupations and hobbyists, from scuba divers to model airplane builders, depend on mixtures. Create a children's alphabet book for mixtures that covers the A to Zs of various mixtures we may encounter each day.

Mixtures Cube

Complete a cube with suggestions and questions to help identify whether a substance is a mixture or a compound. You may choose to put questions or statements on each side of your cube. Use this pattern or create your own cube.

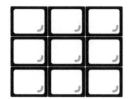

Properties and Changes in Chemistry

Game Show Menu

Objectives Covered Through This Menu and These Activities

- Students will identify the physical and chemical properties of everyday objects.
- Students will identify the characteristics of physical and chemical changes.
- Students will brainstorm and identify examples of physical and chemical changes in their daily lives.

Materials Needed by Students for Completion

- Poster board or large white paper
- Product cube template
- Materials for lab experiment
- Coat hangers (for mobile)
- Index cards (for mobile)
- String (for mobile)
- Ruler (for comic strip)
- Internet access (for WebQuest)
- Magazines (for collage)

Special Notes on the Use of This Menu

This menu allows students to create a WebQuest. There are multiple versions and templates for WebQuests available on the Internet. Teachers should decide whether to specify a certain format or allow students to create one of their own choosing.

Time Frame

- 2–3 weeks—Students are given the menu as the unit is started and the guidelines and point expectations on the back of the menu are discussed. As lessons are taught throughout the unit, students and the teacher can refer back to the options associated with that topic. The teacher will go over all of the options for the topic being covered and have students place checkmarks in the boxes next to the activities they are most interested in completing. As teaching continues throughout the 2–3 weeks, activities are discussed, chosen, and submitted for grading.

- 1 week—At the beginning of the unit, the teacher chooses an activity from each area that he or she feels would be most valuable for students. Stations can be set up in the classroom. These activities are available for student choice throughout the week as regular instruction takes place.
- 1–2 days—The teacher chooses an activity from an objective to use with the entire class during that lesson time.

Suggested Forms

- Lab report rubric
- All-purpose rubric
- Free-choice proposal form for point-based products

Guidelines for the Properties and Changes in Chemistry Game Show Menu

- You must choose at least one activity from each topic area.

- You may not do more than two activities in any one topic area for credit. (You are, of course, welcome to do more than two for your own investigation.)

- Grading will be ongoing, so turn in products as you complete them.

- All free-choice proposals must be turned in and approved *prior* to working on that free choice.

- You must earn 100 points for a 100%. You may earn extra credit up to _____ points.

- You must show your teacher your plan for completion by: _____.

Properties and Changes in Chemistry

Name:_____ Date:_____

Physical Properties	Chemical Properties	Physical Changes	Chemical Changes	Potpourri	Points for Each Level
☐ Design a pamphlet about physical properties. It should include the different properties with everyday examples of each. (15 pts.)	☐ Create a windowpane with examples of different chemical properties. (10 pts.)	☐ Design an acrostic for the words "Physical Changes." Each descriptive phrase should be an example of a physical change you observe on a daily basis. (15 pts.)	☐ Create a mobile with examples of different chemical changes. (10 pts.)	☐ Create a collage with a total of at least 20 examples of physical properties, physical changes, and chemical changes. Label each picture. (15 pts.)	10–15 points
☐ Create a cube with six questions that would help the user identify the physical properties of an object. (20 pts.)	☐ Create a song or rap about how to identify the chemical properties of everyday objects and include examples. (25 pts.)	☐ Many inventions are designed to make life easier. Choose an invention that makes our life easier by completing a physical change. Create an advertisement for that invention. (25 pts.)	☐ Create a comic strip in which a chemical change plays a major role. (25 pts.)	☐ Create a folded quiz book about the differences between changes and properties. (20 pts.)	20–25 points
☐ Design a lab experiment with at least four parts in which participants identify and measure the physical properties of a household object. (30 pts.)	☐ Write and perform a murder mystery play in which the secret to the mystery lies in a knowing about chemical properties. (30 pts.)	☐ Complete a 24-hour physical change diary in which you record *every* physical change you do in the 24-hour period. (30 pts.)	☐ Create a WebQuest on chemical changes. It should include at least one site with a video example of a chemical change. (30 pts.)	☐ Consider the question: Which occurs more often on earth: physical or chemical changes? Write a newspaper article that shares your opinion and includes examples to support your viewpoint. (30 pts.)	30 points
Free Choice (prior approval) (25–50 pts.)	**Free Choice** (prior approval) (25–50 pts.)	**Free Choice** (prior approval) (25–50 pts.)	**Free Choice** (prior approval) (25–50 pts.)	**Free Choice** (prior approval) (25–50 pts.)	25–50 points
Total:	Total:	Total:	Total:	Total:	**Total Grade:**

© Prufrock Press Inc. • *Differentiating Instruction With Menus: Middle School Edition: Science*
This page may be photocopied or reproduced with permission for student use.

67

Physical Properties Cube

Complete a cube with six questions that can help identify the physical properties of an object. Use this pattern or create your own cube.

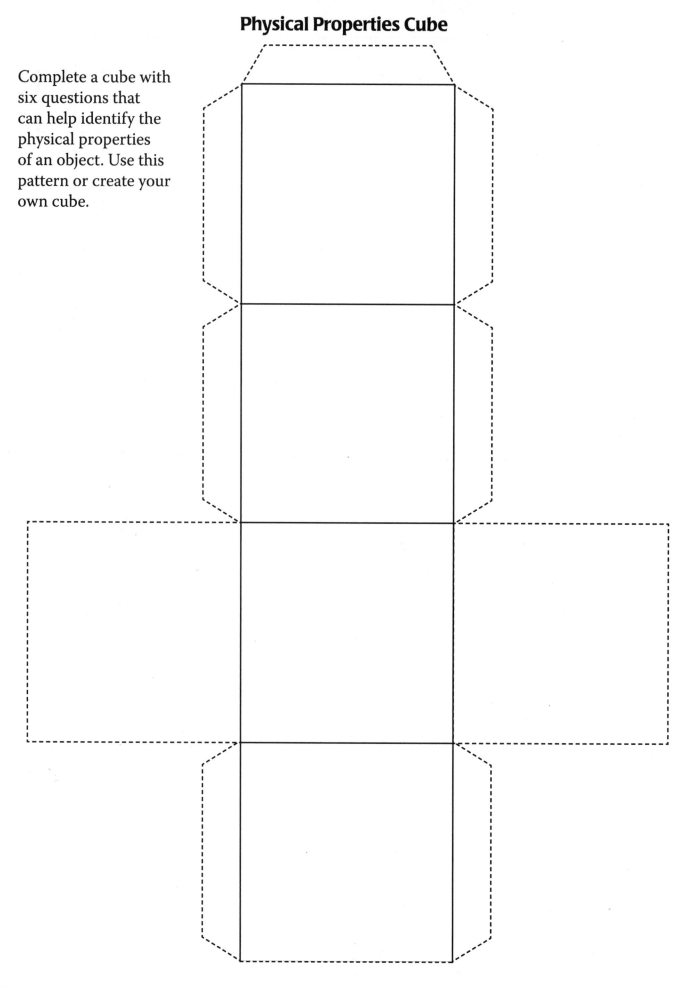

© Prufrock Press Inc. • *Differentiating Instruction With Menus: Middle School Edition: Science*
This page may be photocopied or reproduced with permission for student use.

Chemical Reactions

20-50-80 Menu

Objectives Covered Through This Menu and These Activities
- Students will identify the products and reactants in chemical reactions.
- Students will understand how the Law of Conservation of Mass is related to chemical reactions.
- Students will produce examples of balanced chemical reactions.
- Students will express how to balance chemical reactions.

Materials Needed by Students for Completion
- Poster board or large white paper
- Materials for board games (folders, colored cards, etc.)
- Materials for a class lesson
- Materials for a student-designed experiment

Special Notes on the Use of This Menu
Students are given the option to design and perform their own science experiment. Students may need access to lab equipment and supplies—in which case, it helps to have them submit a list at least 2 days ahead of time to give the teacher plenty of time to gather the necessary materials. It usually is safer for this to be conducted in the classroom or science laboratory, although some students may ask to work on them at home.

Time Frame
- 1–2 weeks—Students are given the menu as the unit is started, and the teacher discusses all of the product options on the menu. As the different options are discussed, students will choose products that add to a total of 100 points. As the lessons progress through the week(s), the teacher and students refer back to the menu options associated with content being taught.
- 1–2 days—The teacher chooses an activity or product from the menu to use with the entire class.

Suggested Forms
- Lab report rubric
- All-purpose rubric
- Free-choice proposal form for point-based products

Chemical Reactions

Directions: Choose two activities from the menu below. The activities must total 100 points. Place a checkmark next to each box to show which activities you will complete. All activities must be completed by _____.

---

20 Points

❏ Write three facts and a fib about products, reactants, or the Law of Conservation of Mass.

❏ Create a windowpane with at least six different examples of chemical reactions.

---

50 Points

❏ Make a song or rap that tells how to complete and balance a chemical reaction.

❏ Design a chemical reaction board game. The question cards should focus on completing and balancing chemical reactions.

❏ Create your own way to teach how to complete and balance chemical reactions. Write up your lesson.

❏ Free choice: Submit a proposal form for a product of your choice.

---

80 Points

❏ Create your own experiment that uses a chemical reaction to demonstration the Law of Conservation of Mass.

❏ Create a children's book that introduces young readers to the chemistry behind the chemical reactions they observe on a daily basis.

Force, Motion, and Newton's Laws

List Menu

Objectives Covered Through This Menu and These Activities

- Students will distinguish between speed and velocity.
- Students will calculate force, speed, and acceleration using real-world applications.
- Students will identify examples of force and Newton's three laws of motion in their daily lives.

Materials Needed by Students for Completion

- Poster board or large white paper
- Microsoft PowerPoint or other slideshow software
- Magazines (for collage)
- Materials for creating a marble roller coaster
- DVD or VHS recorder

Special Notes on the Use of This Menu

This menu allows students the opportunity to create an educational video. Although students enjoy producing their own videos, there often are difficulties obtaining the equipment and scheduling the use of the video recorder. This can be modified by allowing students to act out the educational video (like a play) or, if students have the technology, they may wish to produce a Webcam or Flash version of their video.

Time Frame

- 1–2 weeks—Students are given the menu as the unit is started and the guidelines and point expectations are discussed. Students usually will need to earn 100 points for 100%, although there is an opportunity for extra credit if the teacher would like to use another target number. Because this menu covers one topic in depth, the teacher will go over all of the options on the menu and have students place checkmarks in the boxes next to the activities they are most interested in completing. Teachers will need to set aside a few moments to sign the agreement at the bottom of the page with each student. As instruction continues, activities are completed by students and submitted for grading.
- 1–2 days—The teacher chooses an activity or product from an objective to use with the entire class during that lesson time.

Suggested Forms

- All-purpose rubric
- Free-choice proposal form for point-based products

Name: _____ Date: _____

Force, Motion, and Newton's Laws

Guidelines:
1. You may complete as many of the activities listed within the time period.
2. You may choose any combination of activities.
3. Your goal is 100 points. You may earn up to _____ points extra credit.
4. You may be as creative as you like within the guidelines listed below.
5. You must show your plan to your teacher by _____.
6. Activities may be turned in at any time during the working time period. They will be graded and recorded on this sheet as you continue to work, so keep it safe!

Plan to Do	Activity to Complete	Point Value	Date Completed	Points Earned
	Create a song or rap that explains the difference between speed and velocity.	20		
	Create a windowpane for the 10 most important vocabulary words in this unit.	10		
	Develop a worksheet for calculating force, speed, or acceleration with at least five real-world situations.	20		
	Design a PowerPoint presentation that teaches users how to calculate speed, force, and acceleration.	15		
	Create a collage of pictures that show forces at work in our daily lives. Identify the forces at work in each picture.	10		
	Create a roller coaster with at least three hills and one loop that can transport a marble at least 2 meters from start to finish.	30		
	Create a children's book that teaches young readers about force and Newton's three laws of motion.	30		
	Make a flipbook for Newton's three laws of motion.	10		
	Record an educational video about Newton's three laws of motion and the part they play in our daily lives.	30		
	Physicists have proclaimed that any motion could be an example of all three of Newton's laws of motion, depending on how you interpret the motion. Create a brochure that supports or disproves this statement.	30		
	Develop a unique method for remembering each of Newton's laws. Share your method with your classmates.	30		
	How would Isaac Newton feel about being so famous in today's time? Prepare a "You Be the Person" presentation to answer your classmates' questions about your life and work.	30		
	Submit your free-choice proposal form for a product of your choice.	10–30		
	Total number of points you are planning to earn.	**Total points earned:**		

I am planning to complete _____ activities that could earn up to a total of _____ points.

Teacher's initials _____ Student's signature _____

Energy Transfers

20-50-80 Menu

Objectives Covered Through This Menu and These Activities

- Students will be able to identify and give examples of energy transfers from their daily lives.
- Students will be able to communicate how the Law of Conservation of Energy applies to energy transfers.

Materials Needed by Students for Completion

- Poster board or large white paper
- Blank index cards (for trading cards/card game and mobile)
- Coat hangers (for mobile)
- String (for mobile)
- Materials for student-designed experiment
- Materials for Rube Goldberg machine

Special Notes on the Use of This Menu

Students are given the option to design and perform their own science experiment. Students may need access to lab equipment and supplies—in which case, it helps to have them submit a list at least 2 days ahead of time to give the teacher plenty of time to gather the necessary materials. It usually is safer for this to be conducted in the classroom or science laboratory, although some students may ask to work on them at home.

Time Frame

- 1–2 weeks—Students are given the menu as the unit is started, and the teacher discusses all of the product options on the menu. As the different options are discussed, students will choose products that add to a total of 100 points. As the lessons progress through the week(s), the teacher and students refer back to the menu options associated with content being taught.
- 1–2 days—The teacher chooses an activity or product from the menu to use with the entire class.

Suggested Forms

- Lab report rubric
- All-purpose rubric
- Free-choice proposal form for point-based products

Energy Transfers

Directions: Choose two activities from the menu below. The activities must total 100 points. Place a checkmark next to each box to show which activities you will complete. All activities must be completed by _____.

---

20 Points

❏ Create a set of trading cards for the different types of energy transfers. Be sure to include a real-world example for each.

❏ Design a mobile for at least six different energy transfers, including everyday examples.

---

50 Points

❏ Create a card game that will assist players in understanding how energy can be converted between various objects. Be sure to include the sun!

❏ Design an experiment that demonstrates the Law of Conservation of Energy.

❏ Write and perform a song for younger children to help them understand energy transfers and the law of conservation.

❏ Free choice—submit a proposal form for a product of your choice.

---

80 Points

❏ Food chains control the transfer of energy through an ecosystem. Choose a local food chain and create a PowerPoint presentation to show how the energy is transferred and converted through the system.

❏ Research Rube Goldberg and his machines. Create your own Rube Goldberg machine that can move a marble more than one meter, has at least 10 different parts, and has at least three different energy transfers. Be ready to present your machine and explain the different energy transfers.

```
2
  □ _____
5
  □ _____
  □ _____
  □ _____
8
  □ _____
```

Nuclear Energy

20-50-80 Menu

Objectives Covered Through This Menu and These Activities

- Students will explain how radioactive materials are used to create energy.
- Students will describe the chemical reactions behind the production of nuclear energy.
- Students will explain the uses and importance of radioactive materials.
- Students will investigate the development of radioactive materials and the history of radioactivity.

Materials Needed by Students for Completion

- Poster board or large white paper
- Graph paper or Internet access (for crossword puzzle)
- Materials for three-dimensional timeline
- Materials for board games (folders, colored cards, etc.)

Time Frame

- 1–2 weeks—Students are given the menu as the unit is started, and the teacher discusses all of the product options on the menu. As the different options are discussed, students will choose products that add to a total of 100 points. As the lessons progress through the week(s), the teacher and students refer back to the menu options associated with content being taught.
- 1–2 days—The teacher chooses an activity or product from the menu to use with the entire class.

Suggested Forms

- All-purpose rubric
- Free-choice proposal form for point-based products

Nuclear Energy

Directions: Choose two activities from the menu below. The activities must total 100 points. Place a checkmark next to each box to show which activities you will complete. All activities must be completed by _____.

---

20 Points

❑ Create a crossword puzzle about nuclear energy and radioactive materials.

❑ Write Three Facts and a Fib about how radioactive materials are used to produce nuclear energy.

---

50 Points

❑ Create a questionnaire about the different uses of radioactive material (other than producing energy). Use the responses to write a newspaper editorial that shares what the public knows about radioactive material.

❑ Children often think nuclear power is scary. Create a children's book that presents information about nuclear power in a fun and nonbiased manner.

❑ Create a board game in which players travel through a nuclear power plant answering questions about nuclear power and radioactive materials.

❑ Marie Curie was one of the first scientists who documented radioactivity. Beginning with her works, create a three-dimensional timeline that covers the history of nuclear power and radioactive materials.

---

80 Points

❑ Research how nuclear plants create energy and what information communities consider before allowing a plant to be constructed. Pretend your community is considering having its energy provided by a nuclear power plant. Write a letter to your local newspaper sharing the information gathered through your research and your opinion on the plant.

❑ Write and perform a play about a town that is debating the possibility of a nuclear power plant being built on the outskirts of its community.

Light

Tic-Tac-Toe Menu

Objectives Covered Through This Menu and These Activities

- Students will distinguish between reflection and refraction.
- Students will share examples of optical instruments from their daily lives and how they use light.
- Students will show how concave and convex mirrors reflect light.
- Students will show how concave and convex lenses refract light.

Materials Needed by Students for Completion

- Poster board or large white paper
- Graph paper or Internet access (for crossword puzzle)
- Microsoft PowerPoint or other slideshow software
- Blank index cards (for trading cards)
- Materials for student-created experiments using mirrors and lenses
- Materials for models of reflection and refraction

Special Notes on the Use of This Menu

Students are given the option to design and perform their own science experiment. Students may need access to lab equipment and supplies—in which case, it helps to have them submit a list at least 2 days ahead of time to give the teacher plenty of time to gather the necessary materials. It usually is safer for this to be conducted in the classroom or science laboratory, although some students may ask to work on them at home.

Time Frame

- 2–3 weeks—Students are given the menu as the unit is started. As the teacher presents lessons throughout the week, he or she should refer back to the menu options associated with that content. The teacher will go over all of the options for that content and have students place checkmarks in the boxes that represent the activities they are most interested in completing. As teaching continues over the next 2–3 weeks, activities chosen and completed should make a column or row. When students complete this pattern, they have completed one activity from each content area, learning style, or level of Bloom's, depending on the design of the menu.
- 1 week—At the start of the unit, the teacher chooses the three activities he or she feels are most valuable for the students. Stations can be

set up in the classroom. These three activities are available for student choice throughout the week as regular instruction takes place.

- 1–2 days—The teacher chooses an activity from the menu to use with the entire class.

Suggested Forms

- Lab report rubric
- All-purpose rubric
- Free-choice proposal form

Light

☐ *Reflection and Refraction* Create an experiment that demonstrates reflection and refraction of light using household objects.	☐ *Mirrors and Lenses* Develop a crossword puzzle about the different types of mirrors and lenses and their use in our lives.	☐ *Optical Instruments* Create a PowerPoint presentation that shows examples of various optical instruments and how each uses light. Include a diagram for each instrument that includes the path light follows.
☐ *Optical Instruments* Create a set of trading cards for various instruments that need light. Each card needs to include the location of any mirrors or lenses and how light passes through the instrument.	☐ ***Free Choice: Reflection and Refraction*** (Fill out your proposal form before beginning the free choice!)	☐ *Mirrors and Lenses* Design an experiment that shows how both concave and convex lenses and concave and convex mirrors reflect and refract light.
☐ *Mirrors and Lenses* Create a model that shows how concave and convex mirrors and lenses impact light waves.	☐ *Optical Instruments* Research how various optical instruments use light. Create a working model that shows how one of the instruments uses light.	☐ *Reflection and Refraction* You have been given the following challenge: Through the use of mirrors and/or lenses, could you shine a laser pointer in your classroom and have it show on the wall outside the school's gymnasium? Develop a plan and design an experiment to test the plan!

Check the boxes you plan to complete. They should form a tic-tac-toe across or down.
All products are due by: _____.

Static Electricity

20-50-80 Menu

Objectives Covered Through This Menu and These Activities

- Students will determine how to produce static electricity.
- Students will determine the factors that affect static buildup.
- Students will understand how static electricity is a form of energy.

Materials Needed by Students for Completion

- Poster board or large white paper
- Microsoft PowerPoint or other slideshow software
- Large lined index cards (for recipe cards)
- Materials for creating an electrostatic motor

Special Notes on the Use of This Menu

Students are given the option to design their own electrostatic motor. There are many different designs that can be used to create their motor and multiple Web sites that provide detailed instructions and videos on their construction (insert "electrostatic motor" into an online search engine). In order to build it, students may need access to lab equipment and supplies—in which case, it helps to have them submit a list at least 2 days ahead of time to give the teacher plenty of time to gather the necessary materials.

Time Frame

- 1–2 weeks—Students are given the menu as the unit is started, and the teacher discusses all of the product options on the menu. As the different options are discussed, students will choose products that add to a total of 100 points. As the lessons progress through the week(s), the teacher and students refer back to the menu options associated with content being taught.
- 1–2 days—The teacher chooses an activity or product from the menu to use with the entire class.

Suggested Forms

- All-purpose rubric
- Free-choice proposal form for point-based products

Static Electricity

Directions: Choose two activities from the menu below. The activities must total 100 points. Place a checkmark next to each box to show which activities you will complete. All activities must be completed by _____.

---

20 Points

❑ Using a balloon and a piece of dried cereal, determine six different ways that you can show how static electricity can be produced. Make a poster to show the six different ways you discovered.

❑ Create an acrostic for static electricity with meaningful words and examples.

---

50 Points

❑ Create an advertisement for a household product that reduces static electricity. Include how the product works.

❑ Lightening is considered one big display of static electricity. Create a PowerPoint presentation that shows how this takes place.

❑ You and a friend are having a "shocking" competition. You both want to try to create the biggest static charge, and hence the biggest shock. Create a recipe card for creating the biggest shock naturally (no outlets, electricity, or batteries)!

❑ Free choice—submit a proposal form for a product of your choice.

---

80 Points

❑ Static electricity often is a problem when people brush their hair or take clothes out of the dryer and put them on. Develop a unique product that can be used to solve one of these two problems. This product should be something that is not currently being sold. Be prepared to share your product and how it reduces static electricity.

❑ Investigate the various designs of electrostatic motors. Build your own electrostatic motor. Be sure to seek parent or teacher supervision if needed!

Electricity and Circuits

Tic-Tac-Toe Menu

Objectives Covered Through This Menu and These Activities

- Students will share how to be safe when working with electricity.
- Students will explain different ways in which electricity is produced.
- Students will differentiate between parallel and series circuits.
- Students will determine the uses for parallel and series circuits.

Materials Needed by Students for Completion

- Poster board or large white paper
- Aluminum foil (for quiz board)
- Wires (for quiz board)
- Materials for creating circuits (wire, batteries, small light bulbs)

Time Frame

- 2–3 weeks—Students are given the menu as the unit is started. As the teacher presents lessons throughout the week, he or she should refer back to the menu options associated with that content. The teacher will go over all of the options for that content and have students place checkmarks in the boxes that represent the activities they are most interested in completing. As teaching continues over the next 2–3 weeks, activities chosen and completed should make a column or row. When students complete this pattern, they have completed one activity from each content area, learning style, or level of Bloom's, depending on the design of the menu.
- 1 week—At the start of the unit, the teacher chooses the three activities he or she feels are most valuable for the students. Stations can be set up in the classroom. These three activities are available for student choice throughout the week as regular instruction takes place.
- 1–2 days—The teacher chooses an activity from the menu to use with the entire class.

Suggested Forms

- All-purpose rubric
- Free-choice proposal form

Electricity and Circuits

☐ *Design a Brochure*	☐ *Create a Quiz Board*	☐ *Write a Letter*
Make a brochure that shows how to be safe when using electricity.	Create a quiz board with at least five questions on how electricity is produced. Be sure to make your questions challenging! Have a classmate test your quiz board.	A family friend has heard about a new house wiring option: Simply Series! This allows the entire house to be connected with one series circuit. Using your knowledge about circuits, write a letter to your friend about the new wiring option.
☐ *Build Some Circuits!*	☐ *Free Choice: Electricity Safety* (Fill out your proposal form before beginning the free choice!)	☐ *Design an Advertisement*
Build a working example of a parallel circuit and an example of a series circuit using no more than three batteries in each one.		Choose an energy source currently used to produce electricity and create an advertisement for that energy source. Be sure to include how energy is produced by this source.
☐ *Make a Diagram*	☐ *Make a Poster*	☐ *Perform a Play*
There are various electronics—from flashlights to radios—that can run on electricity produced by hand cranks. Create a cross-cut diagram to show how one of these objects works without being plugged in or using batteries.	Make a poster that shows examples of parallel and series circuits. Use electrical symbols in your drawing.	Write and perform a play that demonstrates how to be safe when working with electricity.

Check the boxes you plan to complete. They should form a tic-tac-toe across or down.
All products are due by: _____.

CHAPTER 7

Life Sciences

Ecosystems

Baseball Menu

Objectives Covered Through This Menu and These Activities

- Students will identify biotic and abiotic factors within an ecosystem.
- Students will describe food chains and food webs found in ecosystems.
- Students will identify examples of interdependence and symbiotic relationships within an ecosystem.
- Students will identify producers, consumers, and predators within an ecosystem.

Materials Needed by Students for Completion

- Poster board or large white paper
- Magazines (for collage)
- Blank index cards (for trading cards)
- Boxes (for diorama)
- Materials for board games (folders, colored cards, etc.)
- Bulletin board display materials
- Internet access (for WebQuest)
- DVD or VHS recorder (news report and mockumentary)

Special Notes on the Use of This Menu

This menu allows students to create a WebQuest. There are multiple versions and templates for WebQuests available on the Internet. Teachers should decide whether to specify a certain format or allow students to create one of their own choosing.

This menu also allows students the opportunity to create a news report or mockumentary. Although students enjoy producing their own videos, there often are difficulties obtaining the equipment and scheduling the use of the video recorder. This can be modified by allowing students to act out the news report or mockumentary (like a play) or, if students have the technology, they may wish to produce a Webcam or Flash version of their news report or mockumentary.

In addition, this menu allows students to create a bulletin board display. Some classrooms may only have one bulletin board, so the teacher can divide the board into sections, or additional classroom wall or hall space can be sectioned off for the creation of these displays. Students can plan their display based on the amount of space they are assigned.

Time Frame

- 2–3 weeks—Students are given the menu as the unit is started and the guidelines and point expectations on the top of the menu are discussed. Usually, students are expected to complete 100 points. Because this menu covers one topic in depth, the teacher will go over all of the options for the topic being covered and have students place check-marks in the boxes next to the activities they are most interested in completing. As instruction continues, activities are completed by students and submitted for grading.
- 1 week—At the beginning of the unit, the teacher chooses 1–2 higher level activities that can be integrated into whole-group instruction throughout the week.
- 1–2 days—The teacher chooses an activity from an objective to use with the entire class during that lesson time.

Suggested Forms

- All-purpose rubric
- Free-choice proposal form for point-based products

Name:_____ Date:_____

Ecosystems

Look through the following choices and decide how you want to make your game add to 100 points. Singles are worth 10, doubles are worth 30, triples are worth 50, and a home run is worth 100. Choose any combination you want. Place a checkmark next to each choice you are going to complete. Make sure that your points equal 100!

These choices are not specific to any one ecosystem or biome. When you decide on your choices, plan on including all of the biomes or ecosystems we are studying in your products. For example, if you complete a product that compares two biomes, then you only have included two biomes.

Singles—10 Points Each

❐ Create an acrostic for a predator from your ecosystem. It should include information about the ecosystem and its food chains.

❐ Create a collage of pictures and words that represent your ecosystem. Include a sentence for each item that explains how it is related to your ecosystem.

❐ Create a set of trading cards for your ecosystem that includes examples of the plants and animals found in your ecosystem.

❐ Design a diorama for your ecosystem that includes at least one complete food chain or food web.

❐ Create Three Facts and a Fib about your ecosystem.

❐ Design a folded quiz book that asks questions about the interdependence and symbiotic relationships found in your ecosystem.

❐ Free choice—prepare a proposal form and submit your idea for approval.

Doubles—30 Points Each

❐ Create a travel brochure that would encourage people to visit your ecosystem. Your brochure should include not only general information about your ecosystem but what is special about your ecosystem, making it worth the trip!

❐ Make an ecosystem board game in which players move through your ecosystem encountering both biotic and abiotic factors and examples of interdependence within the ecosystem.

❐ Because they are at the top of the food chain, predators often are thought of as the most important members of any ecosystem. However, all factors in an ecosystem are important. Complete an interview with a producer found in your ecosystem that asks about its importance.

Doubles—30 Points Each

❏ Create an interactive bulletin board display for your ecosystem that includes specific symbiotic relationships found there.

❏ Design a WebQuest for your ecosystem. It will need to include at least one Web site with a video of an aspect of your ecosystem.

❏ Free choice—prepare a proposal form and submit your idea for approval

Triples—50 Points Each

❏ When a non-native consumer or predator is introduced into an ecosystem, there can be both beneficial and disastrous effects. Research a biome to discover how non-native species can impact an ecosystem. Write a news report that shares your discovery and discusses whether you support and film this practice or not.

❏ Biotic and abiotic factors impact an ecosystem. Which factor has the greatest impact on your ecosystem? Create a brochure about this factor and how the ecosystem would be impacted if that factor ceased to exist.

❏ Create a play that shows the interdependence of the producers, consumers, and predators in your ecosystem and how they interact with their environment. Address the ideas of competition, mutualism, commensalism, and parasitism.

Home Run—100 Points

❏ The local television station has offered you the opportunity to film a "mockumentary" video about a local ecosystem. The station requested that it be an in-depth study that includes details about the interactions of the various food webs, the interdependence between the biotic and abiotic factors, and the symbiotic relationships that exist in the ecosystem. Local biologists also had noted that there was evidence that biological competition was having an impact on a few of the animal populations, so be sure to include information on this as well. Be creative!

I Chose:

_____ Singles (10 points each)

_____ Doubles (30 points each)

_____ Triples (50 points each)

_____ Home Run (100 points)

Cycles and Systems

Tic-Tac-Toe Menu

Objectives Covered Through This Menu and These Activities

- Students will determine the impact of removing one part of a system.
- Students will understand that all systems are part of other systems.
- Students will show that all systems have patterns.

Materials Needed by Students for Completion

- Poster board or large white paper
- DVD or VHS recorder (for public service announcement)
- Blank index cards (for trading cards and mobile)
- Coat hangers (for mobile)
- String (for mobile)
- Materials for model of cycle
- Bulletin board display materials
- Microsoft PowerPoint or other slideshow software

Special Notes on the Use of This Menu

This menu allows students the opportunity to create a public service announcement. Although students enjoy producing their own videos, there often are difficulties obtaining the equipment and scheduling the use of the video recorder. This can be modified by allowing students to act out the public service announcement (like a play) or, if students have the technology, they may wish to produce a Webcam or Flash version of their public service announcement.

This menu also allows students to create a bulletin board display. Some classrooms may only have one bulletin board, so the teacher can divide the board into sections, or additional classroom wall or hall space can be sectioned off for the creation of these displays. Students can plan their display based on the amount of space they are assigned.

Time Frame

- 2–3 weeks—Students are given the menu as the unit is started. As the teacher presents lessons throughout the week, he or she should refer back to the menu options associated with that content. The teacher will go over all of the options for that content and have students place checkmarks in the boxes that represent the activities they are most interested in completing. As teaching continues over the next 2–3 weeks, activities chosen and completed should make a column or row. When students complete this pattern, they have completed one activity from each content area, learning style, or level of Bloom's, depending on the design of the menu.

- 1 week—At the start of the unit, the teacher chooses the three activities he or she feels are most valuable for the students. Stations can be set up in the classroom. These three activities are available for student choice throughout the week as regular instruction takes place.
- 1–2 days—The teacher chooses an activity from the menu to use with the entire class.

Suggested Forms

- Lab report rubric
- All-purpose rubric
- Student-taught lesson rubric
- Free-choice proposal form

Cycles and Systems

☐ *Patterns and Parts*	☐ *Missing Something?*	☐ *Part of a Whole*
Scientists will comment that, once you understand how a cycle or system works, you can understand how all of them work. Create a Venn diagram to compare and contrast your cycle or system to your life cycle.	Hypothesize how your cycle might change if one piece was missing. Create and video a public service announcement about how your cycle or system would be different.	Create a set of trading cards for the parts of your system or cycle. Include the role each plays as well as how it contributes to other cycles and systems.
☐ *Part of a Whole*	☐ **Free Choice: Patterns and Parts**	☐ *Missing Something?*
Create a mobile that shows the parts of your cycle or system and how it is part of at least two others.	(Fill out your proposal form before beginning the free choice!)	Create a model that demonstrates the impact of removing one part or stage in your cycle or system.
☐ *Missing Something?*	☐ *Part of a Whole*	☐ *Patterns and Parts*
Decide which stage or part of your cycle or system is the most important to its success. Create a song or rap about your cycle and its most important part.	Design a bulletin board display that shows how your cycle or system is a part of at least two other cycles or systems.	An important concept in all cycles and systems is equilibrium. Investigate how equilibrium plays a part in your cycle or system. Create a PowerPoint presentation that shares this information.

Check the boxes you plan to complete. They should form a tic-tac-toe across or down.
All products are due by: _____.

My cycle or system for this menu: _____.

Human Body Systems

Baseball Menu

Objectives Covered Through This Menu and These Activities
- Students will identify the different systems within the human body.
- Students will demonstrate how the systems within the human body are interrelated.
- Students will show the functions of the organs within each body system.

Materials Needed by Students for Completion
- Poster board or large white paper
- Blank index cards (for trading cards and mobile)
- Materials for board games (folders, colored cards, etc.)
- Coat hangers (for mobile)
- String (for mobile)
- Product cube template
- Materials for body system model
- DVD or VHS Recorder (for video documentary)

Special Notes on the Use of This Menu
This menu gives students the opportunity to create a video documentary. Although students enjoy producing their own videos, there often are difficulties obtaining the equipment and scheduling the use of the video recorder. This can be modified by allowing students to act out the documentary (like a play) or, if students have the technology, they may wish to produce a Webcam or Flash version of their documentary.

Time Frame
- 2–3 weeks—Students are given the menu as the unit is started and the guidelines and point expectations on the top of the menu are discussed. Usually, students are expected to complete 100 points. Because this menu covers one topic in depth, the teacher will go over all of the options for the topic being covered and have students place checkmarks in the boxes next to the activities they are most interested in completing. As instruction continues, activities are completed by students and submitted for grading.
- 1 week—At the beginning of the unit, the teacher chooses 1–2 higher level activities that can be integrated into whole-group instruction throughout the week.

- 1–2 days—The teacher chooses an activity from an objective to use with the entire class during that lesson time.

Suggested Forms

- Lab report rubric
- All-purpose rubric
- Student-taught lesson rubric
- Free-choice proposal form for point-based products

Human Body Systems

Look through the following choices and decide how you want to make your game add to 100 points. Singles are worth 10, doubles are worth 30, triples are worth 50, and a home run is worth 100. Choose any combination you want. Place a checkmark next to each choice you are going to complete. Make sure that your points equal 100!

These choices are not specific to any one body system. When you decide on your choices, plan on including all of the following systems in your products. For example, if you complete a product that compares two systems, then you can check off two systems.

❑ Digestive System   ❑ Circulatory System
❑ Respiratory System   ❑ Nervous System
❑ Skeletal System   ❑ Muscular System

Singles—10 Points Each

❑ Make a flipbook for two body systems. The flipbook must contain the organs in the system and the function of each.

❑ Create a set of trading cards for the organs within the body system of your choice. Each card should include the functions of the organs as well as other organs that depend on it.

❑ Create a mobile for your body system with all of its organs and their functions, and include at least one organ that your system impacts.

❑ Create a human body system windowpane. It should include all of the systems and what purpose they serve in the human body.

❑ Design an acrostic for your body system. Provide descriptions about the function of the system for each letter.

❑ Create a song with hand motions that shows how your body system works. Share it with the class.

❑ Free choice—prepare a proposal form and submit your idea for approval.

Doubles—30 Points Each

❑ Make a human body board game. It must contain information on all of the body systems and their importance to the health of the body.

❑ Create a body system flipbook. Use one flap for each body system. Draw the system and its organs, and show how it helps the body to function.

❑ Design a product cube that analyzes the body system of your choice in depth.

❑ Build a model of your body system that shows all of the organs. Include labels that share the functions of each organ.

Doubles—30 Points Each

❏ Make an informational pamphlet on your body system and its importance to the body's function.

❏ Develop an advertisement for your body system. Include the functions of the system and its importance.

❏ Free choice—prepare a proposal form and submit your idea for approval.

Triples—50 Points Each

❏ Although all of the systems of the human body are interdependent, which system do you feel is most important? Prepare a persuasive speech that explains and supports your point of view.

❏ Write a journal entry for a day in the life of a body system of your choice. Your day should begin when the body goes to sleep and continue for 24 hours.

❏ Create a children's book that explains how the other body systems rely on the body system of your choice.

❏ Prepare a "You Be the Organ" presentation for your class in which you describe why you are the most important organ in the body. Be sure you let your audience know how all of the other systems depend on you!

❏ Research diseases that can cause damage to your body system. Create a brochure about the common diseases and what can be done to prevent them.

Home Run—100 Points

❏ You have been invited to be the first news reporter to participate in a new nanotechnology that allows people to shrink to super small sizes. In your smaller state, you will be able to travel through the human body and make various stops at organ systems and their organs. Use this opportunity to interview all of the organs about their contribution to their systems, as well as the total health of the body. After deciding the order of your trip and how you would like it to be organized, create a video to document your trip through the body.

I Chose:

_____ Singles (10 points each)

_____ Doubles (30 points each)

_____ Triples (50 points each)

_____ Home Run (100 points)

Human Body Cube

Complete the cube for the human body. Use this pattern or create your own cube. Respond to the questions on each side to analyze your body system in depth.

Describe the importance of your body system.

Tell how your body system compares to another system.

List all of the organs in your body system that impact other systems. Explain their impact.

Discuss what would happen if one of the organs in your body system stopped working.

Name one disease that affects your body system. What are the symptoms?

Do all living organisms need your body system to survive? Why or why not?

Plant and Animal Cells

20-50-80 Menu

Objectives Covered Through This Menu and These Activities

- Students will identify the structures in plant and animal cells.
- Students will compare and contrast plant and animal cells.
- Students will create a wet mount (a microscope slide that uses water to aid in viewing).

Materials Needed by Students for Completion

- Poster board or large white paper
- Graph paper or internet access (for crossword puzzle)
- Materials for board games (folders, colored cards, etc.)
- Materials for wet mount (eye dropper, slides, cover slip, microscope)
- DVD or VHS recorder (for video)
- Material for plant person model

Special Notes on the Use of This Menu

This menu allows students the opportunity to create an educational video. Although students enjoy producing their own videos, there often are difficulties obtaining the equipment and scheduling the use of the video recorder. This can be modified by allowing students to act out the educational video (like a play) or, if students have the technology, they may wish to produce a Webcam or Flash version of their video.

Time Frame

- 1–2 weeks—Students are given the menu as the unit is started, and the teacher discusses all of the product options on the menu. As the different options are discussed, students will choose products that add to a total of 100 points. As the lessons progress through the week(s), the teacher and students refer back to the menu options associated with content being taught.
- 1–2 days—The teacher chooses an activity or product from the menu to use with the entire class.

Suggested Forms

- All-purpose rubric
- Free-choice proposal form for point-based products

Name:_____ Date:_____

Plant and Animal Cells

Directions: Choose two activities from the menu below. The activities must total 100 points. Place a checkmark next to each box to show which activities you will complete. All activities must be completed by _____.

---

20 Points

❏ Create a Venn diagram flipbook that compares and contrasts the structure of plant and animal cells.

❏ Design a plant and animal cell crossword puzzle that focuses on the structural differences between the two types of cells.

---

50 Points

❏ Design a board game in which players travel through either a plant or animal cell traveling from organelle to organelle.

❏ Create a wet mount microscope slide to examine an animal cell (cheek cell) and plant cell (onion cell works well). Create a poster that shows how to create the wet mounts. Draw what you view and label the various structures.

❏ You have been hired by an educational network to produce a video series. The topic of your first episode is plant and animal cells in our daily lives. Create a video of your first episode and share it with the class.

❏ Free choice—prepare a proposal form and submit your idea for approval.

---

80 Points

❏ A plant and animal cell are having a disagreement about which is the more complex cell. Write and present a play that follows their debate and shows who really is the most complex.

❏ There are structures that are found only in plant cells. Investigate the importance of these structures. Design a "plant cell person" who would represent how the human body would be different if it had the structures that plant cells contain. Build a model of your person using everyday objects with an accompanying poster that points out his or her important features.

© Prufrock Press Inc. • *Differentiating Instruction With Menus: Middle School Edition: Science*

This page may be photocopied or reproduced with permission for student use.

99

Photosynthesis

20-50-80 Menu

Objectives Covered Through This Menu and These Activities

- Students will name and describe the steps in the process of photosynthesis.
- Students will identify the compounds needed for photosynthesis to take place.
- Students will understand that photosynthesis is an energy transfer.

Materials Needed by Students for Completion

- Poster board or large white paper
- Blank index cards (for trading cards)
- Microsoft PowerPoint or other slideshow software
- DVD or VHS recorder (for commercial)
- Scrapbooking materials
- Materials for photosynthesis experiment

Special Notes on the Use of This Menu

Students are given the option to design and perform their own science experiment. Students may need access to lab equipment and supplies—in which case, it helps to have them submit a list at least 2 days ahead of time to give the teacher plenty of time to gather the necessary materials. It usually is safer for this to be conducted in the classroom or science laboratory, although some students may ask to work on them at home.

This menu also gives students the opportunity to create a commercial. Although students enjoy producing their own videos, there often are difficulties obtaining the equipment and scheduling the use of the video recorder. This can be modified by allowing students to act out the commercial (like a play) or, if students have the technology, they may wish to produce a Webcam or Flash version of their commercial.

Time Frame

- 1–2 weeks—Students are given the menu as the unit is started, and the teacher discusses all of the product options on the menu. As the different options are discussed, students will choose products that add to a total of 100 points. As the lessons progress through the week(s), the teacher and students refer back to the menu options associated with content being taught.

- 1–2 days—The teacher chooses an activity or product from the menu to use with the entire class.

Suggested Forms

- Lab report rubric
- All-purpose rubric
- Free-choice proposal form for point-based products

Photosynthesis

Directions: Choose two activities from the menu below. The activities must total 100 points. Place a checkmark next to each box to show which activities you will complete. All activities must be completed by _____.

---

20 Points

❏ Make a poster that shows how photosynthesis takes place in an organism.

❏ Create a set of trading cards for all of the key players in the photosynthesis process.

---

50 Points

❏ Using PowerPoint, create a presentation that traces the energy conversions in photosynthesis that take place, from the sun's energy to growth in a plant.

❏ Create a commercial about humans' impact on the process of photosynthesis.

❏ Green, leafy plants are not the only organisms that use photosynthesis to create food. Create a scrapbook for the different types of organisms that use photosynthesis and what structures conduct the photosynthesis

❏ Free choice—prepare a proposal form and submit your idea for approval.

---

80 Points

❏ Write and perform a play about people who have to conduct photosynthesis in order to produce food. Be creative in how their life would be different from ours.

❏ Create an experiment that demonstrates how each component is necessary for photosynthesis to take place.

Levels of Organization

20-50-80 Menu

Objectives Covered Through This Menu and These Activities
- Students will identify examples of the different levels of organization.
- Students will determine how to identify the different levels of organization.
- Students will associate levels of organization with nonliving objects.

Materials Needed by Students for Completion
- Poster board or large white paper
- Blank index cards (for concentration cards and mobile)
- Coat hangers (for mobile)
- String (for mobile)
- Materials for model

Time Frame
- 1–2 weeks—Students are given the menu as the unit is started, and the teacher discusses all of the product options on the menu. As the different options are discussed, students will choose products that add to a total of 100 points. As the lessons progress through the week(s), the teacher and students refer back to the menu options associated with content being taught.
- 1–2 days—The teacher chooses an activity or product from the menu to use with the entire class.

Suggested Forms
- All-purpose rubric
- Free-choice proposal form for point-based products

Levels of Organization

Directions: Choose two activities from the menu below. The activities must total 100 points. Place a checkmark next to each box to show which activities you will complete. All activities must be completed by _____.

---

20 Points

❒ Create a levels of organization flipbook that has a flap for each level.

❒ Brainstorm multiple examples of each level of organization. Create concentration cards for the examples and their levels.

---

50 Points

❒ Choose a living organism (other than a human being) that has four levels of organization. Create a mobile to show the levels of organization within your organism.

❒ Not all organisms have organs. Research an "organless" organism and create a brochure that details the structure of the organism and how it carries out the functions usually associated with organs such as digestion, circulation, excretion, and reproduction.

❒ Create a children's song about an organ system of your choice. Be sure to include the organs of the system and their contribution to the system.

❒ Free choice—prepare a proposal form and submit your idea for approval.

---

80 Points

❒ Find a nonliving object that has at least four levels of organization. Make a model of the object and label each level. Include a paragraph for each level that explains how its function is similar to its corresponding level in living things.

❒ You are a cell in an organism's digestive tissues. The organ systems are debating which one is the most important to the functioning of the organism. Prepare a speech to convince the systems that you are the most important!

Heredity

Tic-Tac-Toe Menu

Objectives Covered Through This Menu and These Activities

- Students will identify genes and chromosomes as parts of genetic material.
- Students will understand the causes of mutations and their impacts on the organism.
- Students will identify dominant and recessive traits.
- Students will be able to explain how genetic material is used in selective breeding, cloning, and genetically modified foods.

Materials Needed by Students for Completion

- Poster board or large white paper
- DVD or VHS recorder (for news report)
- Scrapbooking materials
- Materials for board display
- Microsoft PowerPoint or other slideshow software
- Materials for board games (folders, colored cards, etc.)

Special Notes on the Use of This Menu

This menu allows students the opportunity to create a news report video. Although students enjoy producing their own videos, there often are difficulties obtaining the equipment and scheduling the use of the video recorder. This can be modified by allowing students to act out the news report (like a play) or, if students have the technology, they may wish to produce a Webcam or Flash version of their video.

This menu also allows students to create a bulletin board display. Some classrooms may only have one bulletin board, so the teacher can divide the board into sections, or additional classroom wall or hall space can be sectioned off for the creation of these displays. Students can plan their display based on the amount of space they are assigned.

Time Frame

- 2–3 weeks—Students are given the menu as the unit is started. As the teacher presents lessons throughout the week, he or she should refer back to the menu options associated with that content. The teacher will go over all of the options for that content and have students place checkmarks in the boxes that represent the activities they are most interested in completing. As teaching continues over the next 2–3 weeks, activities chosen and completed should make a column or row. When students complete this pattern, they have completed one activity from each content area, learning style, or level of Bloom's, depending on the design of the menu.

- 1 week—At the start of the unit, the teacher chooses the three activities he or she feels are most valuable for the students. Stations can be set up in the classroom. These three activities are available for student choice throughout the week as regular instruction takes place.
- 1–2 days—The teacher chooses an activity from the menu to use with the entire class.

Suggested Forms

- Lab report rubric
- All-purpose rubric
- Student-taught lesson rubric
- Free-choice proposal form

Name:_____ Date:_____

Heredity

☐ *Genes and Chromosomes* Create a skit or play about the different types of mutations that occur and how they impact genes and chromosomes.	☐ *Dominant and Recessive Traits* Research dominant and recessive traits that humans can display and choose at least 10 traits that interest you. Choose two friends to "cross" and predict what traits their offspring would exhibit. Share your results with the class.	☐ *Changes in Traits* Dog breeders engage in selective breeding in order to improve certain dog breeds. Create a brochure that explains this practice and why it is used.
☐ *Changes in Traits* Farmers and scientists have been working together to develop genetically modified (GM) foods. Create a news report that explains how this is done and shares your view on the creation and use of these "GM" foods.	☐ ***Free Choice: Genes and Chromosomes*** (Fill out your proposal form before beginning the free choice!)	☐ *Dominant and Recessive Traits* Using photos from magazines or photo clipart, create a scrapbook that could represent three generations of a family. Track and share the dominant and recessive traits in each generation on each page.
☐ *Dominant and Recessive Traits* Create a bulletin board display that shows various dominant and recessive traits in a species that was not discussed in class. Include a cross between two of the species that shows how dominant and recessive traits are passed on to offspring.	☐ *Changes in Traits* Cloning has been a genetic reality since 1952 and various organisms have been cloned. Create a PowerPoint presentation on these organisms that addresses how organisms are cloned, the ethical issues behind cloning, and whether you support cloning.	☐ *Genes and Chromosomes* Create a board game that tests your classmates' knowledge of genes, chromosomes, and the mutations that can impact them.

Check the boxes you plan to complete. They should form a tic-tac-toe across or down.

All products are due by: _____.

Mitosis and Meiosis

Tic-Tac-Toe Menu

Objectives Covered Through This Menu and These Activities

- Students will identify the stages of mitosis and meiosis.
- Students will share the significance of the processes of mitosis and meiosis.
- Students will compare and contrast mitosis and meiosis.

Materials Needed by Students for Completion

- Poster board or large white paper
- Materials for board games (folders, colored cards, etc.)
- Ruler (for comic strip)
- Materials for edible meiosis model

Time Frame

- 2–3 weeks—Students are given the menu as the unit is started. As the teacher presents lessons throughout the week, he or she should refer back to the menu options associated with that content. The teacher will go over all of the options for that content and have students place checkmarks in the boxes that represent the activities they are most interested in completing. As teaching continues over the next 2–3 weeks, activities chosen and completed should make a column or row. When students complete this pattern, they have completed one activity from each content area, learning style, or level of Bloom's, depending on the design of the menu.
- 1 week—At the start of the unit, the teacher chooses the three activities he or she feels are most valuable for the students. Stations can be set up in the classroom. These three activities are available for student choice throughout the week as regular instruction takes place.
- 1–2 days—The teacher chooses an activity from the menu to use with the entire class.

Suggested Forms

- All-purpose rubric
- Student-taught lesson rubric
- Free-choice proposal form

Mitosis and Meiosis

☐ *Mitosis*	☐ *Meiosis*	☐ *Comparing Mitosis and Meiosis*
Students have trouble remembering the order of the stages of mitosis and what occurs during each stage. Create a lesson for your class that teaches the stages of mitosis and their importance to the cell.	Meiosis is a multiple-stage cell division process. Create a board game that takes players on a journey through these various stages of meiosis. The questions should focus on the process and its importance in reproductive process.	Some teachers explain that meiosis is actually mitosis happening twice. Is this a correct assumption? Design a poster that shows why a teacher may say that and if it is a true statement.
☐ *Comparing Mitosis and Meiosis*	☐ **Free Choice: Mitosis** (Fill out your proposal form before beginning the free choice!)	☐ *Meiosis*
Write and perform a play in which a chromosome has to choose whether it wants to go through the processes of mitosis and meiosis.		Design an edible model that demonstrates the stages of meiosis. Use only food that can be handled and will not deteriorate.
☐ *Meiosis*	☐ *Comparing Mitosis and Meiosis*	☐ *Mitosis*
Do all cells go through meiosis? Design an informational brochure for the process of meiosis that emphasizes its various stages, which cells experience the process, and its importance to all living things.	Create a comic strip that shows the similarities and differences between mitosis and meiosis in a humorous way.	You have been given the task to interview a centriole about its job and its importance to mitosis. Create your interview questions and provide creative yet reasonable responses to the questions.

Check the boxes you plan to complete. They should form a tic-tac-toe across or down.
All products are due by: _____.

CHAPTER 8

Earth and Space Sciences

Our Atmosphere

20-50-80 Menu

Objectives Covered Through This Menu and These Activities

- Students will identify the layers of the atmosphere and their function.
- Students will identify the composition of the atmosphere and its impact on our lives.

Materials Needed by Students for Completion

- Poster board or large white paper
- Materials for the atmosphere model
- Microsoft Excel
- Internet access (for WebQuest)
- DVD or VHS recorder (for public service announcement, super hero video, or news report)

Special Notes on the Use of This Menu

This menu allows students to create a WebQuest. There are multiple versions and templates for WebQuests available on the Internet. Teachers should decide whether to specify a certain format or allow students to create one of their own choosing.

This menu also gives students the opportunity to create a PSA video. Although students enjoy producing their own videos, there often are difficulties obtaining the equipment and scheduling the use of the video recorder. This can be modified by allowing students to act out the educational video (like a play) or, if students have the technology, they may wish to produce a Webcam or Flash version of their video.

Time Frame

- 1–2 weeks—Students are given the menu as the unit is started, and the teacher discusses all of the product options on the menu. As the different options are discussed, students will choose products that add to a total of 100 points. As the lessons progress through the week(s), the teacher and students refer back to the menu options associated with content being taught.
- 1–2 days—The teacher chooses an activity or product from the menu to use with the entire class.

Suggested Form

•   All-purpose rubric

Name:_____ Date:_____

Our Atmosphere

Directions: Choose two activities from the menu below. The activities must total 100 points. Place a checkmark next to each box to show which activities you will complete. All activities must be completed by _____.

---

20 Points

❏ Create a model of the atmosphere. Include all of its layers. Be creative!

❏ Design a flipbook for the layers of the atmosphere and their composition.

---

50 Points

❏ Use Microsoft Excel to create two pie graphs: one that shows the percentage composition of our atmosphere and one that shows the comparative size of the various layers of the atmosphere.

❏ Venus is considered Earth's sister planet. Create a Venn diagram to compare and contrast the two atmospheres of the two planets.

❏ Many people are "going green" and becoming more concerned about the environment. Considering the layers of the atmosphere, their composition, and their impact on our lives, create a public service announcement that discusses how people can help the atmosphere.

❏ Consider how each layer of the atmosphere impacts the layer directly above and below it. Create a WebQuest that shows the interrelationship between the layers.

---

80 Points

❏ Each layer of the atmosphere serves an important role in our life on Earth's surface. After deciding which layer is the most important, create a news report proclaiming the disappearance of this layer and the effect this will have on our daily lives.

❏ You are the new image consultant for the superhero "Mr. Troposphere." He has this name because his super powers greatly resemble the characteristics of the troposphere. Write a story or create a video about his latest adventure.

© Prufrock Press Inc. • *Differentiating Instruction With Menus: Middle School Edition: Science*

Weather

Tic-Tac-Toe Menu

Objectives Covered Through This Menu and These Activities

- Students will state the function of weather instruments.
- Students will identify the steps of the water cycle and its importance in our daily lives.
- Students will share multiple examples of local weather phenomena and how people can best prepare for them.

Materials Needed by Students for Completion

- Poster board or large white paper
- Microsoft PowerPoint or other slideshow software
- DVD or VHS recorder (for public service announcement)
- Socks (for puppets)
- Paper bags (for puppets)
- Access to the library
- Materials for building weather instrument (varies based on the instrument)

Special Notes on the Use of This Menu

This menu gives students the opportunity to create a public service announcement about local weather phenomena. Although students enjoy producing their own videos, there often are difficulties obtaining the equipment and scheduling the use of the video recorder. This can be modified by allowing students to act out the public service announcement (like a play) or, if students have the technology, they may wish to produce a Webcam or Flash version of their public service announcement.

Time Frame

- 2–3 weeks—Students are given the menu as the unit is started. As the teacher presents lessons throughout the week, he or she should refer back to the menu options associated with that content. The teacher will go over all of the options for that content and have students place checkmarks in the boxes that represent the activities they are most interested in completing. As teaching continues over the next 2–3 weeks, activities chosen and completed should make a column or row. When students complete this pattern, they have completed one activity from each content area, learning style, or level of Bloom's, depending on the design of the menu.

- 1 week—At the start of the unit, the teacher chooses the three activities he or she feels are most valuable for the students. Stations can be set up in the classroom. These three activities are available for student choice throughout the week as regular instruction takes place.
- 1–2 days—The teacher chooses an activity from the menu to use with the entire class.

Suggested Forms

- All-purpose rubric
- Free-choice proposal form

Name:_____ Date:_____

Weather

☐ *Weather Instruments* Your school is thinking of purchasing a school weather station. They have been given a budget of $5,000. Research the different options that are available and create a brochure for the weather station you feel is the best choice.	☐ *The Water Cycle* Create a raindrop puppet. Have the puppet speak about its role in the water cycle and its life as it travels through the water cycle.	☐ *Weather Phenomena* Make a PowerPoint presentation for dangerous weather-related phenomena. Include photos of each and a brief explanation of its cause.
☐ *Weather Phenomena* Design a public service announcement to educate the public about the worst weather phenomena in your area. Include what causes the phenomena, the possible dangers, and the best options for coping with the weather occurrence.	☐ **Free Choice:** **Weather Instruments** (Fill out your proposal form before beginning the free choice!)	☐ *The Water Cycle* Research the ways in which people in your community can impact the water cycle. Write a newspaper article that helps the people in your community understand their impact on the water cycle.
☐ *The Water Cycle* Create a water cycle song that a second-grade teacher could use with her students as she teaches them about the water cycle.	☐ *Weather Phenomena* Visit your local library to investigate the many books available on different weather phenomena. Choose the book(s) that you feel represent the information in the best way. Make a list of all of the books you previewed and write a paragraph that tells why the books you chose were the best.	☐ *Weather Instruments* Build your own working weather instrument. Use it to record data about your local weather for at least a week. Include instructions on how you constructed the instrument.

Check the boxes you plan to complete. They should form a tic-tac-toe across or down.
All products are due by: _____.

Rocks and Minerals

List Menu

Objectives Covered Through This Menu and These Activities
- Students will identify the different types of rocks.
- Students will state the processes of the rock cycle.
- Students will understand that rocks are made of minerals.

Materials Needed by Students for Completion
- Poster board or large white paper
- Product cube template
- Magazines (for collage)
- Materials for board games (folders, colored cards, etc.)
- Graph paper or Internet access (for crossword puzzle)
- Scrapbooking materials
- Blank index cards (for trading cards)
- Large lined index cards (for recipe cards)
- Materials for bulletin board display

Special Notes on the Use of This Menu
This menu allows students to create a bulletin board display. Some classrooms may only have one bulletin board, so the teacher can divide the board into sections, or additional classroom wall or hall space can be sectioned off for the creation of these displays. Students can plan their display based on the amount of space they are assigned.

Time Frame
- 1–2 weeks—Students are given the menu as the unit is started and the guidelines and point expectations are discussed. Students usually will need to earn 100 points for 100%, although there is an opportunity for extra credit if the teacher would like to use another target number. Because this menu covers one topic in depth, the teacher will go over all of the options on the menu and have students place checkmarks in the boxes next to the activities they are most interested in completing. Teachers will need to set aside a few moments to sign the agreement at the bottom of the page with each student. As instruction continues, activities are completed by students and submitted for grading.
- 1–2 days—The teacher chooses an activity or product from an objective to use with the entire class during that lesson time.

Suggested Forms
- All-purpose rubric
- Free-choice proposal form for point-based products

Name:_____ Date:_____

Rocks and Minerals

Guidelines:
1. You may complete as many of the activities listed within the time period.
2. You may choose any combination of activities.
3. Your goal is 100 points. You may earn up to _____ points extra credit.
4. You may be as creative as you like within the guidelines listed below.
5. You must show your plan to your teacher by _____.
6. Activities may be turned in at any time during the working time period. They will be graded and recorded on this sheet as you continue to work, so keep it safe!

Plan to Do	Activity to Complete	Point Value	Date Completed	Points Earned
	Create a rock product cube that studies one type of rock in depth.	20		
	Make an acrostic for sedimentary, igneous, and metamorphic rocks.	15		
	Make a collage of household items that are made from minerals and their products.	15		
	Visit the school's library. After looking at all of the books on rocks and the rock cycle, choose the one you like best and develop a new book cover for it.	25		
	Design a rock cycle game that focuses on the types of rocks and how they are formed.	25		
	Make a crossword puzzle for rocks and their properties.	15		
	Write and perform a rock cycle song or rap.	30		
	Create a scrapbook for a piece of obsidian. The scrapbook should focus on what it was before it was obsidian, as well as how and where it was created.	15		
	Write a recipe card for creating a metamorphic rock of your choice. Start with its minerals!	15		
	You are a piece of sandstone that really wants to become gneiss. Write and perform a play that documents your journey.	30		
	Design a bulletin board display to teach your classmates about the rock cycle and the types of rocks that can be created.	25		
	Write Three Facts and a Fib about how a sedimentary rock is formed.	20		
	Create a greeting card for the birth of quartzite.	20		
	Create a set of trading cards for different igneous, sedimentary, and metamorphic rocks.	15		
	Submit your free-choice proposal form for a product of your choice.	10–30		
	Total number of points you are planning to earn.	**Total points earned:**		

I am planning to complete ____ activities that could earn up to a total of ____ points.

Teacher's initials _____ Student's signature _____

Rocks and Minerals Cube

Use this pattern or create your own cube. After choosing one type of rock (sedimentary, igneous, or metamorphic), analyze it further by answering the following questions on each side of the cube.

List at least 5 examples of this type of rock.

Explain how your type of rock is created.

Discuss your rock type's importance in the rock cycle.

Explain how your rock type is dependent on minerals.

Choose your favorite rock. Explain what makes it your favorite.

Place a color picture of your favorite type of rock on this side.

Structure of the Earth

20-50-80 Menu

Objectives Covered Through This Menu and These Activities

*   Students will list the layers of the Earth and the varying compositions of each layer.
*   Students will discuss the development of the layers of the Earth and how each layer has impacted humans on the crust.
*   Students evaluate the feasibility of humans traveling to Earth's core.

Materials Needed by Students for Completion

*   Poster board or large white paper
*   Microsoft PowerPoint or other slideshow software
*   Materials for board games (folders, colored cards, etc.)
*   Large blank lined index cards (for recipe cards)

Time Frame

*   1–2 weeks—Students are given the menu as the unit is started, and the teacher discusses all of the product options on the menu. As the different options are discussed, students will choose products that add to a total of 100 points. As the lessons progress through the week(s), the teacher and students refer back to the menu options associated with content being taught.
*   1–2 days—The teacher chooses an activity or product from the menu to use with the entire class.

Suggested Forms

*   All-purpose rubric
*   Free-choice proposal form for point-based products

Structure of the Earth

Directions: Choose two activities from the menu below. The activities must total 100 points. Place a checkmark next to each box to show which activities you will complete. All activities must be completed by _____.

20 Points

❏ Create a folded quiz book about the structure of the Earth and how each layer was created.

❏ Design a PowerPoint presentation that shows how the Earth is structured and how its structure impacts our life on its surface.

50 Points

❏ Create a children's book that teaches the reader about the composition of the various layers of the earth and the theories behind their development.

❏ Create a board game in which players journey through the various layers of the Earth answering questions about its structure, composition, and importance.

❏ Considering the composition and organization of the Earth's structure, create a recipe card for our Earth.

❏ Free choice—prepare a proposal form and submit your idea for approval.

80 Points

❏ Create a list of books and movies that focus on journeying to the center of the Earth. Choose one to study in depth. Write a newspaper article about the book or movie discussing which aspects were scientifically accurate and which were fiction.

❏ Write and perform a play about a journey to the center of the Earth. The play should be based as closely on scientific fact as possible.

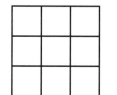

Earth's History

Tic-Tac-Toe Menu

Objectives Covered Through This Menu and These Activities

- Students will describe how fossils are formed.
- Students will differentiate between relative and absolute dating.
- Students will understand the Law of Superposition and how it is used in dating fossils.

Materials Needed by Students for Completion

- Poster board or large white paper
- Materials for archeological dig box (box, string, and artifacts)
- Materials for model of soil layers
- Large lined index cards (for instruction cards)
- Materials for bulletin board display

Special Notes on the Use of This Menu

This menu allows students to create a bulletin board display. Some classrooms may only have one bulletin board, so the teacher can divide the board into sections, or additional classroom wall or hall space can be sectioned off for the creation of these displays. Students can plan their display based on the amount of space they are assigned.

Time Frame

- 2–3 weeks—Students are given the menu as the unit is started. As the teacher presents lessons throughout the week, he or she should refer back to the menu options associated with that content. The teacher will go over all of the options for that content and have students place checkmarks in the boxes that represent the activities they are most interested in completing. As teaching continues over the next 2–3 weeks, activities chosen and completed should make a column or row. When students complete this pattern, they have completed one activity from each content area, learning style, or level of Bloom's, depending on the design of the menu.
- 1 week—At the start of the unit, the teacher chooses the three activities he or she feels are most valuable for the students. Stations can be set up in the classroom. These three activities are available for student choice throughout the week as regular instruction takes place.

- 1–2 days—The teacher chooses an activity from the menu to use with the entire class.

Suggested Forms

- All-purpose rubric
- Student-taught lesson rubric
- Free-choice proposal form

Name:_____ Date:_____

Earth's History

☐ **Fossils** Research archeological digs. Using your information, create an archeological dig in a box with at least five realistic artifacts. Provide instructions on how to use the box including creating a grid, labeling, and cataloging the "finds."	☐ **Law of Superposition** Make a poster that shows at least five layers of sedimentation with fossils in each layer. Create Three Facts and a Fib to accompany your poster.	☐ **Relative vs. Absolute Dating** A geologist has stated that one of the oldest fossils on record has been found. She has calculated its age to be 62,530 years old. Are these findings realistic? Write a letter to this geologist about her findings and your support or disagreement using your knowledge of geologic dating.
☐ **Relative vs. Absolute Dating** Create a brochure on relative and absolute dating. Include how dating is conducted and its importance in the study of geology.	☐ **Free Choice: Fossils** (Fill out your proposal form before beginning the free choice!)	☐ **Law of Superposition** Research the composition and layers of the soil in our area. Create a cross-cut model of these layers. Include a paragraph about how your model relates to the Law of Superposition.
☐ **Law of Superposition** Create an instruction card that shows how to use the Law of Superposition to determine the age of a fossil in a rock layer.	☐ **Relative vs. Absolute Dating** Research relative and absolute dating techniques. Create a bulletin board display that shows the limitations of each type and how these techniques are used by scientists.	☐ **Fossils** Design a lesson for your classmates on the different types of fossils and how they are formed.

Check the boxes you plan to complete. They should form a tic-tac-toe across or down.

All products are due by: _____.

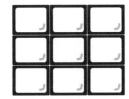

Constructive and Destructive Forces

Game Show Menu

Objectives Covered Through This Menu and These Activities

- Students will compare and contrast weathering and erosion.
- Students will name agents of erosion and types of weathering.
- Students will identify landforms created through deposition.
- Students will show the different types of faults.
- Students will express what causes earthquakes and how scientists locate their epicenter.
- Students will describe how the different types of volcanoes and mountains are formed.

Materials Needed by Students for Completion

- Poster board or large white paper
- Materials for model of local weathering
- Materials for model of different types of faults
- Materials for bridge model
- DVD or VHS recorder (for news report)
- Coat hangers (for mobile)
- Index cards (for mobile)
- String (for mobile)
- Materials for demonstration about deposition
- Ruler (for comic strip)
- Graph paper or Internet access (for crossword puzzle)
- Scrapbooking materials

Special Notes on the Use of This Menu

This menu gives students the opportunity to create a video news report. Although students enjoy producing their own videos, there often are difficulties obtaining the equipment and scheduling the use of the video recorder. This can be modified by allowing students to act out the news report (like a play) or, if students have the technology, they may wish to produce a Webcam or Flash version of their news report.

Time Frame

- 2–3 weeks—Students are given the menu as the unit is started and the guidelines and point expectations on the back of the menu are discussed. As lessons are taught throughout the unit, students and the teacher can refer back to the options associated with that topic. The teacher will go over all of the options for the topic being covered and have students place checkmarks in the boxes next to the activities they are most interested in completing. As teaching continues throughout the 2–3 weeks, activities are discussed, chosen, and submitted for grading.

- 1 week—At the beginning of the unit, the teacher chooses an activity from each area that he or she feels would be most valuable for his or her students. Stations can be set up in the classroom. These activities are available for student choice throughout the week as regular instruction takes place.
- 1–2 days—The teacher chooses an activity from an objective to use with the entire class during that lesson time.

Suggested Forms

- All-purpose rubric
- Student-taught lesson rubric
- Free-choice proposal form for point-based products

Guidelines for the Constructive and Destructive Forces Game Show Menu

- You must choose at least one activity from each topic area.

- You may not do more than two activities in any one topic area for credit. (You are, of course, welcome to do more than two for your own investigation.)

- Grading will be ongoing, so turn in products as you complete them.

- All free-choice proposals must be turned in and approved *prior* to working on that free choice.

- You must earn 120 points for a 100%. You may earn extra credit up to _____ points.

- You must show your teacher your plan for completion by: _____.

Constructive and Destructive Forces

	Tier 1	Tier 2	Tier 3	Free Choice	Total
Weathering and Erosion	☐ Make a Venn diagram that compares and contrasts weathering and erosion. (15 pts.)	☐ Create a model that shows the agents of erosion and types of weathering that occur in your area. (20 pts.)	☐ Create a news report that exposes a local problem with either weathering or erosion. Be sure to include pictures or video to document the problem. (30 pts.)	**Free Choice** (prior approval) (25–50 pts.)	Total:
Deposition	☐ Make a mobile that shows various landforms that are created by deposition. (10 pts.)	☐ Design a demonstration that shows how deposition takes place. (20 pts.)	☐ Research the creation and changes of the Mississippi Delta over time. Using your data, make a poster that predicts how the delta will change during the next 30 years. (30 pts.)	**Free Choice** (prior approval) (25–50 pts.)	Total:
Faults	☐ Create a model that shows the different types of faults. (15 pts.)	☐ Create an advertisement for a subdivision of new homes being built on a fault line. (20 pts.)	☐ The word *fault* has multiple meanings. Write and perform a play in which the main character constantly confuses the meanings, possibly with disastrous results. (30 pts.)	**Free Choice** (prior approval) (25–50 pts.)	Total:
Earthquakes	☐ Create a brochure that explains what causes earthquakes and includes earthquake safety tips. (15 pts.)	☐ Scientists use triangulation to locate the epicenter of an earthquake. Create a lesson for your classmates that teaches them how to locate an epicenter. (25 pts.)	☐ Design and build a bridge model that could withstand a major seismic event. (30 pts.)	**Free Choice** (prior approval) (25–50 pts.)	Total:
Volcanoes	☐ Make a poster that shows the different ways that volcanoes are formed and classified. (10 pts.)	☐ Create a comic strip that shows how volcanoes are related to the ring of fire. (25 pts.)	☐ Write a letter to your teacher explaining which is more dangerous: earthquakes or volcanoes. Support your opinion with facts. (30 pts.)	**Free Choice** (prior approval) (25–50 pts.)	Total:
Mountains	☐ Make a flipbook that shows how different types of mountains are formed. Include examples of where each type is located. (10 pts.)	☐ Design a crossword puzzle on mountains, their origin, and their locations in the world. (20 pts.)	☐ A family has made it their goal to visit the five most majestic mountains in the world. Create a scrapbook that documents the family's journeys. Include how each mountain was formed and why it was chosen. (30 pts.)	**Free Choice** (prior approval) (25–50 pts.)	Total:
Points for Each Level	10–15 points	20–25 points	30 points	25–50 points	**Total Grade:**

Our Universe

Tic-Tac-Toe Menu

Objectives Covered Through This Menu and These Activities

- Students will describe the locations, relative sizes, and properties of various objects in space.
- Students will investigate and evaluate the theories of the origin of the universe.
- Students will compute and express the distances in space.

Materials Needed by Students for Completion

- Poster board or large white paper
- Blank index cards (for trading cards)
- DVD or VHS recorder (for video documentary)
- Microsoft PowerPoint or other slideshow software
- Materials for board games (folders, colored cards, etc.)
- Materials for three-dimensional timeline

Special Notes on the Use of This Menu

This menu gives students the opportunity to create a video documentary. Although students enjoy producing their own videos, there often are difficulties obtaining the equipment and scheduling the use of the video recorder. This can be modified by allowing students to act out the documentary (like a play) or, if students have the technology, they may wish to produce a Webcam or Flash version of their documentary.

Time Frame

- 2–3 weeks—Students are given the menu as the unit is started. As the teacher presents lessons throughout the week, he or she should refer back to the menu options associated with that content. The teacher will go over all of the options for that content and have students place checkmarks in the boxes that represent the activities they are most interested in completing. As teaching continues over the next 2–3 weeks, activities chosen and completed should make a column or row. When students complete this pattern, they have completed one activity from each content area, learning style, or level of Bloom's, depending on the design of the menu.
- 1 week—At the start of the unit, the teacher chooses the three activities he or she feels are most valuable for the students. Stations can be

set up in the classroom. These three activities are available for student choice throughout the week as regular instruction takes place.
- 1–2 days—The teacher chooses an activity from the menu to use with the entire class.

Suggested Forms
- All-purpose rubric
- Student-taught lesson rubric
- Free-choice proposal form

Our Universe

☐ *Objects in Space* Research the various objects found in the universe. Create a set of trading cards for the objects. Be sure to include a scale that shows the differences in the relative sizes of the object.	☐ *Measuring Distances* Develop a class lesson that teaches your classmates about how distance is measured in space. Be sure your lesson includes how to take the large distances and make the numbers more manageable.	☐ *The Origins of Our Universe* Create Three Facts and a Fib about the theories behind the origins of our universe.
☐ *The Origins of Our Universe* Research the various theories that explain the origins of our universe. Choose the theory that you believe is best supported and write a children's book about the theory.	☐ **Free Choice: Objects in Space** (Fill out your proposal form before beginning the free choice!)	☐ *Measuring Distances* Many scientists would like to develop a plan to send astronauts to our closest planet, Mars. Research the considerations (including the time needed) for making this trip. Use this information to make a video documentary about the idea of humans traveling within our solar system.
☐ *Measuring Distances* Investigate how the distances in space are calculated and the units used to record them. Design a PowerPoint presentation that shares the information you discovered.	☐ *The Origins of Our Universe* After researching the various theories of the origins of the universe, develop a three-dimensional timeline that documents the important events in the changing of our universe's structure.	☐ *Objects in Space* Create a universe board game in which participants travel to at least six different objects found in our universe. Questions need to focus on the properties of the different destinations.

Check the boxes you plan to complete. They should form a tic-tac-toe across or down.

All products are due by: _____.

Our Solar System

Tic-Tac-Toe Menu

Objective Covered Through This Menu and These Activities

- Students will express the properties of inner planets, outer planets, and other bodies in space that make each unique.

Materials Needed by Students for Completion

- Poster board or large white paper
- Scrapbooking materials
- DVD or VHS recorder (for science video and commercial)

Special Notes on the Use of This Menu

This menu gives students the opportunity to create a science video or commercial. Although students enjoy producing their own videos, there often are difficulties obtaining the equipment and scheduling the use of the video recorder. This can be modified by allowing students to act out the video or commercial (like a play) or, if students have the technology, they may wish to produce a Webcam or Flash version of their video or commercial.

Time Frame

- 2–3 weeks—Students are given the menu as the unit is started. As the teacher presents lessons throughout the week, he or she should refer back to the menu options associated with that content. The teacher will go over all of the options for that content and have students place checkmarks in the boxes that represent the activities they are most interested in completing. As teaching continues over the next 2–3 weeks, activities chosen and completed should make a column or row. When students complete this pattern, they have completed one activity from each content area, learning style, or level of Bloom's, depending on the design of the menu.
- 1 week—At the start of the unit, the teacher chooses the three activities he or she feels are most valuable for the students. Stations can be set up in the classroom. These three activities are available for student choice throughout the week as regular instruction takes place.
- 1–2 days—The teacher chooses an activity from the menu to use with the entire class.

Suggested Forms

- All-purpose rubric
- Free-choice proposal form

Our Solar System

☐ *The Outer Planets* Create a drawing or model of an alien that could survive on one of the outer planets in our solar system. Label all adaptations and how they help with its survival.	☐ *Other Bodies in Our Solar System* You have decided to take a journey through our solar system but can only visit a comet, meteor, or asteroid. Create a scrapbook for your journey, and include why you chose that body over the others.	☐ *The Inner Planets* Write and perform a play in which the main characters are the inner planets. Be sure the characteristics of each planet come through in the play.
☐ *The Inner Planets* Develop an informational science video on the inner planets and their characteristics.	☐ **Free Choice: The Outer Planets** (Fill out your proposal form before beginning the free choice!)	☐ *Other Bodies in Our Solar System* Create Three Facts and a Fib about meteors, meteorites, and meteoroids.
☐ *Other Bodies in Our Solar System* A new space book is being published called *Space Rocks!* It is about the various rocks in space: comets, meteors, meteoroids, and meteorites. Create a book cover for this new book.	☐ *The Inner Planets* A space travel company has decided to offer "inner planet" trips. Create a commercial promoting the various inner planet destinations.	☐ *The Outer Planets* The president has decided to make a space colony on one of the outer planets. Create an argument for the planet he should choose and why. State your argument in a letter to the president.

Check the boxes you plan to complete. They should form a tic-tac-toe across or down.

All products are due by: _____.

References

Anderson, L. (Ed.), Krathwohl, D. (Ed.), Airasian, P., Cruikshank, K., Mayer, R., Pintrich, P., et al. (2001). *A taxonomy for learning, teaching, and assessing: A revision of Bloom's taxonomy of educational objectives* (Complete ed.). New York: Longman.

Keen, D. (2001). *Talent in the new millennium: Report on year one of the programme.* Retrieved August 29, 2008, from http://www.aare.edu.au/01pap/kee01007.htm

About the Author

After teaching science for more than 15 years, both overseas and in the U.S., Laurie E. Westphal now works as an independent gifted education and science consultant. She enjoys developing and presenting staff development on differentiation for various districts and conferences, working with teachers to assist them in planning and developing lessons to meet the needs of their advanced students.

Laurie currently resides in Houston, TX, and has made it her goal to share her vision for real-world, product-based lessons that help all students become critical thinkers and effective problem solvers. She is the author of the *Differentiating Instruction With Menus* series as well as *Hands-On Physical Science* and *Science Dictionary for Kids*.